Music

How It Came To Be What It Is

HANNAH SMITH

CAMBRIDGE UNIVERSITY PRESS

Cambridge, New York, Melbourne, Madrid, Cape Town,
Singapore, São Paolo, Delhi, Tokyo, Mexico City

Published in the United States of America by Cambridge University Press, New York

www.cambridge.org
Information on this title: www.cambridge.org/9781108038812

© in this compilation Cambridge University Press 2011

This edition first published 1898
This digitally printed version 2011

ISBN 978-1-108-03881-2 Paperback

This book reproduces the text of the original edition. The content and language reflect
the beliefs, practices and terminology of their time, and have not been updated.

Cambridge University Press wishes to make clear that the book, unless originally published
by Cambridge, is not being republished by, in association or collaboration with, or
with the endorsement or approval of, the original publisher or its successors in title.

CAMBRIDGE LIBRARY COLLECTION

Books of enduring scholarly value

Music

The systematic academic study of music gave rise to works of description, analysis and criticism, by composers and performers, philosophers and anthropologists, historians and teachers, and by a new kind of scholar - the musicologist. This series makes available a range of significant works encompassing all aspects of the developing discipline.

Music

Hannah Smith (1849–1939) was a composer for children and an educator. In 1903 she published the popular *Founders of Music*, a series of biographical sketches of composers written for children. Written in 1898, when Wagner had been dead for only fifteen years, this is a concise history of music and instruments, aimed at the enthusiast. Covering broad subjects rather than concentrating on a few composers, Smith discusses not just the development of musical styles but also how musical notation developed, how the ear functions and how musical instruments produce the sounds they do. The tastes of the time are evident, particularly in the surprisingly detailed discussion of the Oratorio: however, the book allows us to see how music and its progress were regarded at the turn of the twentieth century, before composers such as Stravinsky and Schoenberg shook the musical establishment.

Cambridge University Press has long been a pioneer in the reissuing of out-of-print titles from its own backlist, producing digital reprints of books that are still sought after by scholars and students but could not be reprinted economically using traditional technology. The Cambridge Library Collection extends this activity to a wider range of books which are still of importance to researchers and professionals, either for the source material they contain, or as landmarks in the history of their academic discipline.

Drawing from the world-renowned collections in the Cambridge University Library, and guided by the advice of experts in each subject area, Cambridge University Press is using state-of-the-art scanning machines in its own Printing House to capture the content of each book selected for inclusion. The files are processed to give a consistently clear, crisp image, and the books finished to the high quality standard for which the Press is recognised around the world. The latest print-on-demand technology ensures that the books will remain available indefinitely, and that orders for single or multiple copies can quickly be supplied.

The Cambridge Library Collection will bring back to life books of enduring scholarly value (including out-of-copyright works originally issued by other publishers) across a wide range of disciplines in the humanities and social sciences and in science and technology.

MUSIC

HOW IT CAME TO BE WHAT IT IS

MUSIC

HOW IT CAME TO BE
WHAT IT IS

BY

HANNAH SMITH

ILLUSTRATED

LONDON
JOHN MURRAY, ALBEMARLE STREET
1898

TO

MY FATHER

PREFACE

THIS little book is founded upon various courses of lectures which the writer has given before audiences of students and amateurs during the past few years. To put them into this form it has been necessary to make many changes. Something has been added and much omitted. What could easily be made clear by practical musical illustration has had to be explained by mere words and an occasional reference to a familiar composition, and where the treatment of a difficult subject—that of temperament, for instance—could in a lecture be aided by an adjustable chart, it has been necessary to forego such aid and trust to verbal explanation alone.

All reference to individual composers has been omitted, save as they have directly influenced the development of the art, and the aim throughout has been to trace the growth of music as concisely as possible—however, by mere statement of facts, but also by indicating the causes which have led to results—explaining everything so thoroughly and yet so simply that the reader with no more technical knowledge of the art than is necessary to comprehend a few notes may be able to follow intelligently the course of its development. There is, of course, nothing of original research or criticism; but most of the standard works on the subject have been read, or consulted, and the knowledge thus acquired condensed into as few words as possible.

If the result shall aid any lovers of good music toward a more intelligent hearing—which is sure to bring an increased love for the art—the writer will be more than satisfied.

CONTENTS

INTRODUCTION
PAGE
MUSICAL ACOUSTICS 3

CHAPTER I
ANCIENT MUSIC 15

CHAPTER II
MEDIÆVAL MUSIC 26

CHAPTER III
THE BELGIAN SCHOOL 54

CHAPTER IV
MUSIC IN ITALY 68

CHAPTER V
EVOLUTION OF THE MODERN SCALE 75

CHAPTER VI
THE OPERA 83

CHAPTER VII
THE ORATORIO 112

CHAPTER VIII
INSTRUMENTAL MUSIC 121

CHAPTER IX
PRECURSORS OF THE PIANO-FORTE 148

CHAPTER X
DEVELOPMENT OF PIANO-FORTE PLAYING . . . 176

CHAPTER XI
THE ORCHESTRA 200

Music

INTRODUCTION
Musical Acoustics

ALL sounds are the result of atmospheric vibrations. The difference between musical tone and mere sound, or noise, is that the vibrations which produce the former are regular, while those that produce the latter are irregular, or confused.

The reason why some combinations of tones are more agreeable than others is that more undulations of the sound-waves coincide. The octave of any tone has two undulations to one—that is, every other wave of the higher tone fits into one of the lower. The fifth has three waves to every two—that is, every third wave of the higher tone coincides with one of the lower; the fourth has four to three, and so on.

In combinations which are excessively dissonant, as C and C sharp, none of the undulations coincide. If two sounds of equal intensity can be so produced—as is possible—that the elevations of one wave exactly coin-

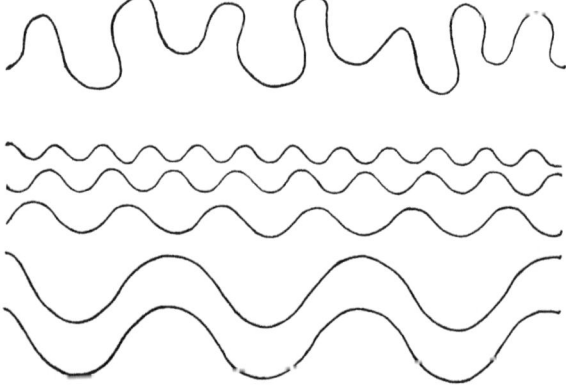

cide with the depressions of the other, the result is silence.

The regular vibrations which produce musical tone may be excited either by forcing air through a tube, by agitating a string in a state of tension, or by striking a resonant body, such as a bell; and upon one or another of these principles every musical instrument is constructed. Strings, however, require to be associated with an elastic, sonorous body, called a sound-board, which takes up the comparatively feeble vibrations produced by

Musical Acoustics 5

the string and communicates them through its entire surface to the surrounding air.

The pitch of a musical tone depends upon the rapidity of the vibrations. Very slow vibrations do not affect the auditory nerve, and the pitch, or acuteness, of the sound increases in direct proportion to the number of vibrations in a given time.

The human ear can perceive tones ranging from about sixteen vibrations in a second * to nearly forty thousand — more than eleven octaves—but only about seven octaves are used in music; the musical character of both highest and lowest extreme tones being very imperfect. There is a very ingenious little instrument, called a syren, which measures exactly the number of vibrations of a given tone. It consists, in its simplest form, of a tube through which air can be forced in a steady current, the tube ending in a box, which is air-tight save for sixteen small holes around the top at equal distances apart. A tightly fitted cover, pierced to correspond, is made to revolve at a regular speed, so that when the holes are opposite one another the air escapes in a series of little puffs; and

---
* Below that number the vibrations may be perceived as sound, but not as continuous tone.

when the cover of the box revolves once in a second, producing sixteen successive and regular puffs of air in that space of time, this series of pulsations gives the lowest C of the great organ. When the cover revolves twice in a second, giving thirty-two puffs or vibrations, we hear the C an octave above; four revolutions, sixty-four vibrations, give the C an octave above that, etc.; and in this manner, by means of a registering apparatus, the number of vibrations required to produce any tone may be exactly determined.

The force, or loudness, of a musical tone depends upon the size, or amplitude, of the vibrations; the greater the breadth of the sound-waves the louder the sound. The quality, or timbre, depends, according to Helmholtz, upon the proportion of harmonics or overtones combined with the principal or fundamental tone.

When a string is made to vibrate, during the vibration of the whole length, the halves, thirds, quarters, etc., also at the same time vibrate independently, producing in rapid succession certain sounds which are called its harmonics, upper partials, or overtones—the tone produced by the whole length of the string being termed the prime, fundamental, or generator. The vibration of the whole length is followed by that of the halves, producing the octave to the fundamental tone;

then by that of the thirds, producing the fifth to that octave; then by the quarters, producing the double octave, and so on.

This series of overtones is called the harmonic chord, and every tone that can be sounded is the generator of such a series. It is the fundamental, or prime, which most strikes the ear, that determines the pitch and intensity of the tone; it is the overtones, or harmonics, combining with it in different proportions, that determine its quality.

With the ear close to the strings of a grand piano it is possible to hear, faintly sounding, this series of harmonics, or overtones; but it is possible also to reveal their presence more distinctly. When any string of the piano is sounded, all the other strings, or parts of strings, which are related to it through its harmonic chord, begin to vibrate in sympathy—that is, if they are freed from the dampers which usually prevent such vibrations. If the keys C, G, c, e, g, b♭, are struck in succession, the tone ceases the instant the finger leaves the key, but if first, by carefully pressing down the key without striking it, the damper is raised from the C C string, which gives the fundamental tone of this series, all these tones will be heard prolonged as harmonics of the longer string. A proof that these tones are really sympathetic vibrations of the harmonic divisions of the fundamental or generator, is this—that they cease the instant the damper falls upon the longer string. Another proof is, that if the same string is freed from the damper and an unrelated series is sounded (C♯, G♯, c♯, e♯, g♯, b, for instance), there is no response.

The influence of harmonics upon the quality of musical tone explains how the touch of a piano-forte player is able to affect the quality of the tone produced, even though the finger has after the first moment of impact no longer any control of the hammer. The overtones develop in regular order from the lowest to the highest, and the first five harmonize with the fundamental tone and add to its beauty.

The higher harmonics, on the contrary, are dissonant, and their admixture produces a harsh quality of tone. A hard, stiff blow of the hammer on the string develops the overtones rapidly, so that the upper, dissonant harmonics are heard before the fundamental tone dies away; while an elastic blow, with flexible muscles, develops the overtones more slowly, and the sound vanishes before the high, dissonant harmonics are heard. Piano-forte manufacturers endeavor to eliminate these dissonant overtones by making the hammer strike the string at a node, or point where the string divides itself into vibrating sections, and by various other mechanical devices; but the touch of the player, also, is an important factor in determining the quality of the tone produced.

The overtones obtained from the strings of a violin are so powerful that they are almost as commonly used as the natural tones of the instrument. The fundamental tone may be extinguished by lightly touching the string at a node, and entire passages are written by composers to be played with harmonics alone. Even from the strings of a grand piano it is possible to obtain this effect, though the tones are fainter. If, by carefully depressing the key, the middle $\bar{c}$ string is freed from the damper, and the e and $\bar{g}$ above and the c an octave below are sounded together, the harmonic $\bar{\bar{g}}$ will be distinctly heard. If—with the same key still pressed down—$\bar{f}$ and $\bar{a}$ above and the F below the bass staff are struck, the harmonic $\bar{\bar{c}}$ will be heard; and in this manner an entire melody may be played with harmonics.

This series of overtones is produced also by a column of air vibrating in a pipe or tube; and these harmonics are the natural tones of all instruments which consist of tubes without pistons or valves—being obtained by simply blowing with greater or less force into the mouth-piece.

The organ by which we become conscious of these vibrations—the human ear—is the most wonderful of all musical instruments. Back of the membrane called the drum, which receives the vibrations, and the series of little bones which transmit them, is an exquisitely sensitive arrangement of nerve-fibres —a tiny harp of three thousand strings, each tuned to a different pitch. These are affected by external vibrations, just as the strings of a violoncello, or piano, are made to vibrate by sympathetic tones of sufficient strength on any other instrument near by. When the sound-waves enter the ear, the tiny string that is tuned to the pitch of the sound that is heard begins to vibrate in sympathy, and communicates its motion to the nerve which carries it to the brain. With this marvellous instrument we are able to separate sounds that come to us all in confusion, and by training and attention we can compel our minds to listen to those we wish to hear and be almost deaf to the others.

The limits of hearing vary very much in different persons. Some ears recognize sounds in what is to others absolute silence;

and even within the limits of the average human ear there are abnormal organs which are capable of perceiving what might almost be called inaudible sounds, and are at the same time deaf to sounds which are audible to everyone else within their reach. The writer has personally known a boy who played the violin with pleasure, but was absolutely deaf to the song of a bird—who knew when a bell was rung by hearing the vibration of the wire that was pulled, but was quite unconscious of the sound of the gong.

This inability to distinguish particular shades of sound, which is quite distinct from deafness, and seems to correspond to color-blindness of the eye, is probably the result of an imperfection in the delicate arrangement of sympathetic nerve-fibres which has just been described. Some of the tiny strings of the little harps are lacking; and perhaps such a physical disability may explain also the absence of what is called an ear for music.

The faculty of hearing is susceptible of cultivation and development, just as are the faculties of sight and mental perception. Travellers tell us that the lowest savages cannot distinguish colors, and perceive nothing in a picture but a piece of paper with marks on it; and teachers who labor for the education of such races consider that a great advance has been made when eye and brain acquire the power of recognizing in such representations even the most familiar natural objects. In the same manner the ear requires cultivation; and just as the crudest and most glaring pictorial art is the first to be recognized and enjoyed by the eye of primitive man, so the first sounds that delight his ear are those which to a more refined and cultivated sense often seem harsh and disagreeable. The aim of musicians throughout all time has been to arrange tones in succession and combination so as to give pleasure to their hearers, but the ears of those hearers have always had to be educated to perceive beauty where the keener instinct of the musician assured him it was to be found. The early composers had no guide but this instinct; they simply experimented until they obtained satisfactory results. They knew nothing of the physical facts and scientific principles involved, but the researches of modern science have completely justified their experiments.

The evolution of the arts which appeal to eye and ear may possibly have begun simultaneously, but that which appeals to the hearing, being more subtle and having no necessary connection with practical life, was in its development soon distanced by painting, sculpture, and architecture, which had already attained their highest perfection while music was yet in its cradle. The design of this little book is to trace the growth of this youngest child of the gods in such a way as to give to the general reader, who does not care to follow it in works of greater volume and more detail, some intelligent idea of how music came to be what it is to-day.

I

Ancient Music

THE history of music should begin, probably, with the history of mankind; but the beginnings of the art, as of the race, are shrouded by the impenetrable mists which preceded the dawn of civilization. The myths and fables, however, concerning music are among the most ancient, and the art was always regarded as of divine origin.

When men first built temples and dwellings, they copied the columns and arches of the trees, and the roofs of the caverns in which they had lived. The first painters and sculptors found their models in all natural objects. But the first musicians—how did they begin? Nature, though full of musical sounds, has almost nothing that we can strictly call music. Bird-songs, which give us so much pleasure by their beautiful tones, have seldom anything like a melody that can be written down in musical notation. Musical tones are sounds resulting from atmospheric vibrations which are both regular and rapid. Music is the succession and combination of such tones arranged by art.

Since the human voice is older than any instrument, the first music was, of course, exclusively vocal. The theory has been advanced that, as inarticulate sounds of varying pitch, quality, and intensity are the natural expression of emotion, men sang before they talked; and it is a fact that the least civilized tribes of which we have any knowledge, those whose articulate language is the most limited, have always some rude songs or chants expressive of grief and triumph. But musical sounds are not exactly music. To be music they must have regularly graduated pitch and rhythm. Now the feeling for rhythm— that is, the regular recurrence of accents—is almost universal, and one of the earliest to find expression. The baby claps its hands and moves its body in time to a tune with well-marked accents, and the undeveloped races of people whom we call savages find the same sort of pleasure in the same thing. They have all some rude instrument, drum

Ancient Music   17

or gong, with which they mark the rhythm, or accent, and to the accompaniment of which they dance and sing; and something of this kind was probably the first musical instrument.

But all nations which have ever so little of culture or development have definite melodies, and in the very earliest ages of which we have any record they had also instruments capable of playing such melodies. The fables and stories which antedate history tell of the charm that was wrought upon beasts and trees and stones when Orpheus played before them, and of Pan with his pipes, and of Apollo's lyre.*

Kouie, a Chinese musician who lived a thousand years before Orpheus, said: "When I play upon my kin the animals range themselves before me spellbound with melody;" and in one of the first chapters of the Bible Jubal is mentioned as the father of all those that handle the harp and the organ. Now, what were all these instruments, and how did they come to have them?

---

* It is noticeable that in these myths and fables the wind instruments, pipe and flute, were always associated with shepherds, fauns, and satyrs, while the stringed instruments belonged to gods and poets.

Probably the first idea of a wind instrument was suggested by the breezes whistling through broken reeds; and when it was no‑ 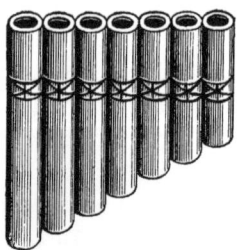 ticed that shorter reeds gave higher, and longer ones lower, tones, it would not require a great deal of cleverness to bind together a row of reeds of different lengths, so graduated as to produce a short musical scale. Such an instrument, called a syrinx, or Pan's pipes, was probably Jubal's organ, and it is from this simple arrangement of reeds or pipes that the modern organ has been developed. Tradition says that Mercury, finding that the filaments of dried skin stretched across the shell of a tortoise produced musical tones, took this as the model for the first stringed instrument— the lyre.

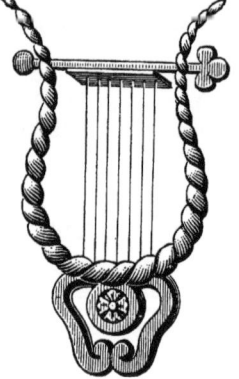

More probably stringed instruments originated in this way. In the early dawn of the arts, when the poet recounted the great deeds of the nation's heroes, and the hunters and warriors in their excitement twanged their bowstrings by way of emphasis and approval, someone noticed that strings of different lengths and drawn more or less tightly gave forth sounds of different pitch; and so, perhaps, Apollo's bow was metamorphosed into Apollo's lyre.

From the monumental remains of Egypt and Asia, which are the oldest records of human civilization, we know that the art of music was early associated both with religion and with domestic life. On the walls of tombs and temples are numerous representations of instruments, both wind and stringed, and bands of players and singers under leaders; but of the music itself there is no record.

The Hebrew music is frequently mentioned in the Bible, but we have no certain knowledge of its character. It was probably founded upon that of Egypt, and its introduction was very likely the result of the training which Moses received in "all the wisdom of the Egyptians." We know that for the temple service there were regularly trained singers under leaders, and that they had various instruments, both wind and stringed; but no authentic melodies have been preserved. Probably they were not written down at all, but taught orally, and so passed on by one generation of singers to the next.

The Greeks, also, probably derived the rudiments of their musical art from the Egyptians. So much has been written by their authors upon the subject, that theoretically we know very well what Greek music was; but about its practice we know very little. It seems to have been chiefly a sort of musical declamation—something between the recitative in an opera and the chants in the church service—accompanied by a few tones from the lyre and flute. In the Greek drama the language was sung, or intoned, not spoken. The theatres were enormous, roofless amphitheatres, seating thousands of persons, and ordinary spoken words could scarcely have been heard. The performers even wore masks with metal mouth-pieces to add to the resonance. The poet was also the composer of the music (the Greek word is the same for both *), and, although Greek music consisted of melody only, the system was so elaborate that years of training were necessary to master its complications.

---

* The musician (musikós) was the *performer*.

Ancient Music

The Greeks had a system of musical notation, but, unfortunately, all the compositions of their most brilliant period—four or five hundred years B.C.—have been lost or destroyed. They used the letters of their alphabet to represent musical sounds, but varied them in many ways—dividing, inverting, turning them to right or left, etc.; and these characters were written directly above the poetical text to which they were to be sung.

The Greek scales were quite different from our modern ones. They were composed of tetrachords—groups of four consecutive notes comprising two whole tones, or steps, and a diatonic half-tone, or step*— and two tetrachords joined together formed a scale. A modern scale also comprises two tetrachords, but the difference is this: the Greek tetrachords were not all alike—in some the half-step came between the third and fourth sounds, in some between the second and third, in others between the first and second—

* Diatonic means, literally, through the tones. A diatonic semitone or half-step is one which is represented by two degrees of the staff—two letters—as E F or F♯ G; whereas a chromatic semitone or half-step is represented on one degree of the staff—by one letter—as F F♯, G G♭, etc.

whereas in a modern scale, no matter where it begins, by the use of sharps or flats the semitones, or half-steps, are made always to fall between the same degrees—

in the major scale between the third and fourth, and seventh and eighth degrees—that is, between the third and fourth degrees of the second tetrachord, so that the two tetrachords precisely correspond. Scales of one octave beginning on each of the white keys of the piano-forte key-board, leaving out all flats and sharps, give an approximately correct idea of the Greek scales. Our modern major or minor scales differ among themselves only in respect to pitch—the intervals follow in the same order, but some scales are higher or lower than others—but each of the Greek scales (or modes, as they were called) had a character of its own, and a distinctive name. The one beginning on D

was the Dorian (which Plato recommends to use chiefly in the education of youth, because of its severe and heroic character); that beginning on E

was the Phrygian; that beginning on F

the Lydian (called the mode of soft complaint, and considered effeminate); the one beginning on G

was the Mixolydian; that beginning on A

the Æolian ("suitable to pleasure, love, and good cheer"); that beginning on B

the Locrian, and the one beginning on C

(corresponding to the modern scale of C major) was the Ionian.* Each scale (excepting

---

* Lucien says: "Each species of harmony" (by harmony the ancients understood what we call melody) "should main-

the last) not only differs from the modern major and minor scales, but differs also from each of the other Greek scales; so that Greek melodies must have been very different from modern ones, and with these scales harmonies, successions of chords such as are now used, would have been impossible.

Besides the diatonic, the Greeks had also chromatic and enharmonic scales; the latter comprising intervals smaller than a semitone, third and quarter tones, like the scales that are still used by Oriental nations. Music composed with such small intervals would seem to us simply out of tune. But Greek music, like that of the Orientals, was founded upon melody—upon tones in succession, not sounded together in harmony—and cannot be judged by our standard. The development of Oriental music has been limited exclusively to melody, and the history of modern music is really the history of the European development of the art. Harmony, as we understand it, is a product of the Occident, and comprehensible only by Occidental civilization. To Oriental ears European

---

tain its own character; the Phrygian, its enthusiasm—the Lydian, its convivial tone—the Dorian, its solemnity—the Ionian, its gaiety."

harmonies are positively distasteful. The best Oriental melodies have, however, if we do not insist upon measuring them by our standard, a charm and beauty of their own; and it is impossible to believe that a people with so keen an artistic sense as that with which the ancient Greeks were endowed, should not have found more beauty in their music than is apparent to us in the few authentic specimens that have come down to our time. Some mediocre compositions of the second century—composed long after the Greeks as a nation had passed their prime—one or two fragments, and the hymn to Apollo, more than two thousand years old, which was found quite recently at Delphi, and is by far the most interesting and important known specimen of Greek musical art, are all that have been preserved. Greek music can be understood only in its connection with poetry, from which it was never intended to be separated—the life and beauty of the melody being dependent upon the poetic rhythm. With the rhythms we are still familiar, but the melodies to which the poet-composers of ancient Greece wedded their immortal verse have vanished forever.

II

Mediæval Music

THE history of the European development of the art of music begins in the fourth century of our era with the establishment in Rome of schools for the training of choristers. When the Church emerged triumphant from the darkness of persecution, and her service was conformed to a definite ritual, the simple song of the early Christians seemed incongruous; and about the middle of the fourth century a church council forbade congregational singing, and prescribed that only the ordered singers in their appointed place should take part in the service. From this time the choir became a distinct feature of ecclesiastical architecture, and singing schools, which were at the same time orphan asylums (orphanotropia), were established in Rome; at first one for the whole city, but afterward each of the greater Roman churches had its own school. The instruction was limited to what was necessary for the church service, and the method of singing was probably antiphonal ; as this, according to Pliny, was customary among the early Christians.

Toward the close of the fourth century St. Ambrose, Archbishop of Milan, selected the four diatonic scales known as the authentic modes, and decreed that upon these all church melodies should be constructed. These scales were, apparently, selected because of their severe religious character. In the heathen temples and theatres other scales and chromatic music were used, but these were forbidden to the Church.

If tradition may be trusted, it was Gregory the Great who, two centuries later, added the four scales which are called the plagal modes;* and in these eight scales, known as the Gregorian modes or tones, were written the Gregorian chants which are

---

* It is thought to have been Gregory who named the tones after the first seven letters of the Roman alphabet, and as the lowest tone of the first of the plagal scales, which he introduced, is A, this would explain why this tone has the first letter of the alphabet.

still sung in Roman and Episcopal churches. These scales were named from the Greek scales upon which they are founded; the plagal, ranging a fourth lower than the authentic, being distinguished by the prefix hypo.

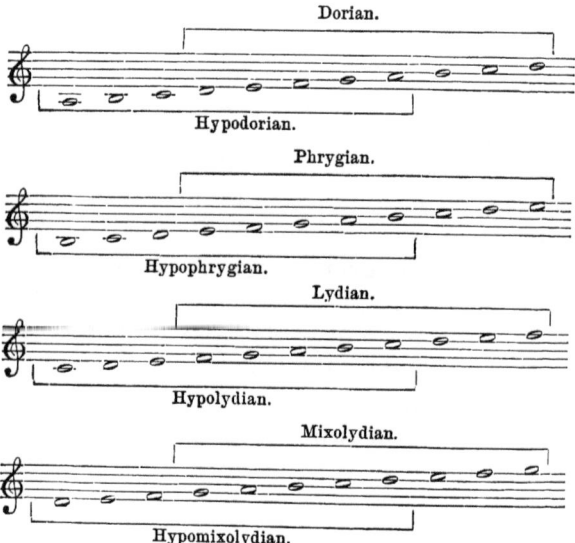

The plagal and authentic scales differ in more than their range—which, indeed, is in some cases identical. The Dorian mode, authentic, and the Mixolydian, plagal, both range from D to D, and in both the semitones fall between the second and third, and

sixth and seventh degrees. But the *final* of
the latter mode—that is, the tone on which
the melody seems to rest, and on which it
almost always closes (corresponding to the
modern tonic)—lies in the middle of the series; whereas in the Dorian mode, authentic,
it is at the beginning. So that while the
Dorian mode, authentic, would be from D,
the final or tonic, to its octave, the Mixoly-

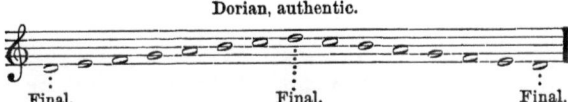
Dorian, authentic.
Final.   Final.   Final.

dian, plagal, would begin on G, its final or
tonic, and extend a fifth above and a fourth
below.

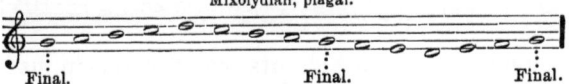
Mixolydian, plagal.
Final.   Final.   Final.

The plagal and authentic forms differ very
much in character—plagal melodies being
generally quieter and less decided than those
in the authentic forms—and this difference
was always recognized by mediæval writers,
who characterized all these scales by special
adjectives. The same difference, as regards
character, exists also between the plagal and

authentic forms of modern scales. The Old Hundredth is a plagal melody, with the tonic

in the middle of its range, and this vigorous old tune (Antioch) is authentic, ranging from tonic to tonic.

The Gregorian chants were soon in use all over Christendom. Trained singers and teachers were sent from Rome to found and encourage a pure style of church music in other countries, and variations from the established system were restrained by ecclesiastical authority.

The organ—but not by any means such an instrument as that with which we are familiar—was probably first used in the church service in the seventh century. In early days the organ was quite a common musical instrument. There were little organs, called portatives, hung by a strap around the neck and played with one hand while the other managed the wind-supply by a bellows; and larger ones, called positives and regals, which were played with both hands while the wind was pumped in by the feet of the player, or by another person; and still larger ones that required several persons to supply the wind. The organ in Winchester Cathedral, which was built in the tenth century, had four hundred pipes and twenty-six bellows, the management of which required seventy strong men* and two players, although the instrument had but ten keys.

The earliest organs had no key-boards, but were played by means of slides which, being pulled out or pushed in, admitted the wind to the pipes or shut it off; and these slides were marked with letters corresponding to the tone of the pipe. Toward the end of the tenth century huge keys, or rather levers,

---

* Who, as the monk who describes the instrument naïvely observes, "perspired uncommonly by the exertion, and encouraged one another to persevere in the work."

were substituted for the slides; and this was the first step toward the key-board which has since been applied, not only to the organ, but to a long line of instruments culminating in the modern grand piano-forte. These keys —which also were often lettered—were four or five inches wide, and were played by means of hard blows with the gloved fist, or even by pressure with the elbows. Of course, on such an instrument there could be no real playing. It was only possible to produce single tones to accompany the chants, or plain song, as they were called, in unison. It was not until the fourteenth century that an organ was constructed on which playing, in any sense of the word, was really possible.

The first attempts to record musical sounds were by the use of letters, and the earliest known musical symbols are the first eight letters of the Greek alphabet. But as Greek music became more and more elaborate the whole alphabet was soon exhausted, so that it was necessary to modify the letters by accents and changes of position; and the system became finally exceedingly complicated, comprising, theoretically at least, almost fifteen hundred different characters. These characters, which were written directly above the poetic text, indicated only the pitch of the melody; the rhythm of Greek music being determined by the rhythm of the poetry.

The Greek system was succeeded by the much simpler use of Roman letters applied in alphabetical order to the degrees of the scale; and these letters are still used as names for those degrees and for the lines and spaces of the staff. Letters were used in notation till about the eighth century, when they were superseded by an entirely new series of characters called 'neumæ.' These neumæ were written, as the letters had been, above the syllables to which they were to be sung, but in such a manner as to indicate the rise and fall of the melody. This was an improvement; but as the neumæ indicated the pitch less definitely than the letters, they were

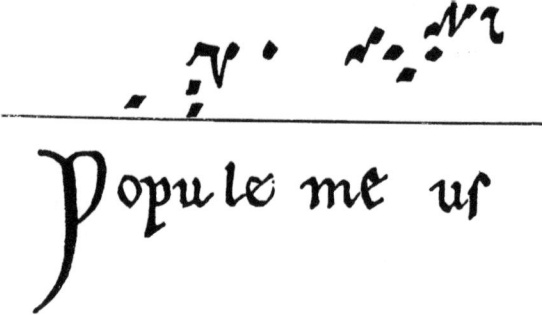

a less certain guide as to the interval by which the voice was to ascend or descend. But about the beginning of the tenth century a

still greater improvement was introduced. A long, red line was drawn horizontally across the parchment, and all neumæ placed directly upon this line were understood to represent the note F; the highest F in the bass of our modern system. The position of one note being thus absolutely fixed, that of all the others was rendered much more definite; and this new plan met with so much favor that a yellow line, to represent C (middle C of the piano-forte key-board), was soon added. When the lines were drawn in black, the letters F and C were placed at the beginning, and so originated the clef signatures,

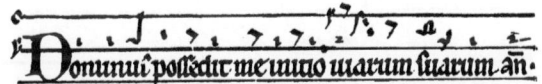

which are merely modifications of the old Gothic letters.

VARIOUS FORMS OF THE F CLEF

VARIOUS FORMS OF THE C CLEF

VARIOUS FORMS OF THE G CLEF

In the tenth century a Flemish monk named Hucbald, or Hucbaldus, introduced a greater number of lines; writing the syllables to be sung in the spaces between them and the letter T or S (tonus or semitonus) at the be-

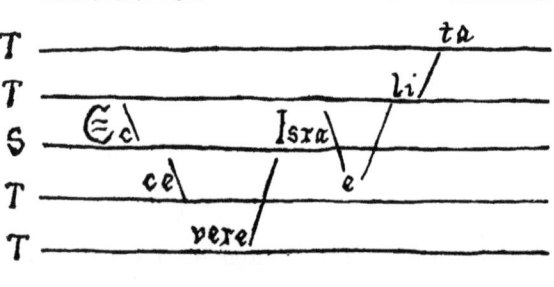

ginning of each line, to show whether the interval was a tone or a semitone. About the same time, also, another stave was invented, the spaces of which were left vacant; the

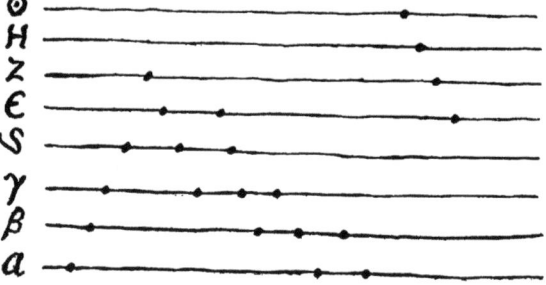

notes being indicated by points or dots upon the lines, and the actual degrees of the scale by Greek letters at the beginning. The combination and modification of these ideas seem to have resulted in drawing a four-lined stave and writing the neumæ on alternate lines and spaces.

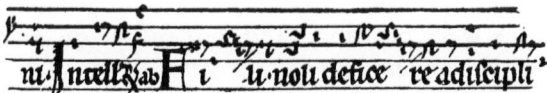

This invention is generally, though without sufficient proof, ascribed to Guido d'Arezzo —a Benedictine monk who lived in the eleventh century—to whose book, the 'Micrologus,' we are indebted for much information concerning the music of his time. Guido, who was a practical musician with a decided talent for teaching, aroused much jealousy and dislike among his fellow-teachers by his superior cleverness and openly expressed dissatisfaction with their methods. "When the little boys," says Guido, "have finally learned to read the Psalter, they can read all other books, and even the common laborers learn their work once for all—whoever has once trimmed a vine or planted a tree will be able to do it again as well, or better; these wonderful singing teachers, however, and their scholars may sing every day for a hundred years and yet will not be able to sing the smallest response without instruction. How can anyone who cannot sing a new melody correctly at sight call himself a singer or musician?"—and in another place: "In the church service it often sounds, not as if we were praising God, but rather quarrelling among ourselves."

Guido set to work to establish a better method of teaching, and in a month's time the boys were able to sing at sight absolutely new melodies — to the great amazement of the hearers. His envious and jealous fellow-monks, however, succeeded in having Guido formally expelled from the convent; but after a time the pope, having heard of his wonderful new system of teaching, invited him to Rome. Guido explained his method so successfully that the pope himself was able to sing at sight a musical phrase, and Guido was invited to remain in Rome and found a singing school for the clergy. Unfortunately, however, he could not endure the Roman climate; he fell ill and had to leave the city. But after being so honored by the head of the Church he thought it a favorable moment to

Mediæval Music 39

return to his convent; and this time, as he naïvely, or sarcastically, remarks, the abbot was convinced of the excellence of his methods—all of which we know from Guido's letters to his friend, Brother Michael.

In one of these letters he explains the method of teaching which made him so famous. "If," he says, "you would commit any sound or neuma to memory, to the end that whensoever you may wish, in whatsoever melody, whether known to you or unknown, it may quickly present itself so that you may at once enunciate it without any doubt, you must note that sound or neuma in the beginning of some well-known tune. And because for the purpose of retaining every sound in the memory after this manner it is necessary to have ready a melody which begins with that same sound, I have used the melody which follows for teaching children from first to last."* "You see, therefore," continues

* Hymn to St. John the Baptist. (Eighth century.)

Guido, "that this melody begins as to its six divisions with six different sounds. He, then, who through practice can attain the power of leading off with certainty the beginning of each division, will be in a position to strike these six sounds easily wheresoever he may meet with them."

It is difficult for us, who have always at hand instruments of fixed intonation to give the singer the desired pitch, to realize the value of this device. But down to the end of the sixteenth century, unaccompanied vocal music was the rule in the service of the Italian Church, and, as confusion and false starts arising from uncertainty in regard to pitch would have been most indecorous in the conduct of a religious service, it was indispensable that a chorister should be able infallibly to sound Ut, Re, Mi, Fa, Sol and La without the aid of any instrument whatever.

Guido, who was the most progressive musician of his time, rearranged the scale itself in hexachords—groups of six consecutive

Mediæval Music 41

sounds with a diatonic semitone between the third and fourth, the remaining intervals being whole tones. The hexachords began on G, C and F, and in order to bring the semitone of the latter hexachord between its third and fourth sounds the note B was made flat. This

seems to be the first step toward that uniformity in the position of the semitones which is characteristic of the modern scales. For a long time the flat was applied only to this note B, to soften the harshness of the tritone —the series of three consecutive whole tones, or steps, which occurs between F and B of the natural scale. The sharp was not used until the thirteenth century.

The sounds of which these hexachords are composed were sung to the syllables Ut, Re, Mi, Fa, Sol and La,* the semitones always

---

* When the hexachord was discarded in favor of the octave the syllable Si was added to the others, and about two centuries ago Do was substituted for Ut—the use of the latter syllable having been discontinued in every country excepting France.

falling between Mi and Fa. But in addition to these syllables the notes were named also by letters, as at present, and the letters and syllables did not always correspond. Fa, Sol and La (C, D, E,) of one hexachord corresponded to Do, Re, Mi (C, D, E,) of another.

The art of so changing the syllables, when a melody extended from one hexachord into the next, as to bring the semitone always between Mi and Fa, was called solmization; and this art was of the greatest importance in the training of a mediæval musician. From the beginning this system involved great difficulties, which constantly increased with the introduction of chromatic intervals and the addition of higher and lower tones. Various efforts were made to simplify the study of music, but several centuries elapsed before the hexachords were finally abandoned for the simpler system of the octave and nomenclature of the alphabet.

The method of writing on alternate lines and spaces was soon generally adopted, but without any limit to the number of lines. In early manuscripts are staves of six, eight, twelve, or even more, but as the inconven-

ience of these became apparent the number was gradually reduced to four or five. The Gregorian tones, or plain-chant, are still written on a stave of four lines, and our modern piano-forte stave seems to be a modification of the great stave of eleven lines.

If the broken line which is used for the C between the bass and treble staves were continuous, we should have this eleven-lined stave. The C clef would be upon this line, and the names of the notes the same as at present. For convenience in reading, however, this middle line is omitted, a section of it being used when required, and in piano-forte music the C clef does not appear; though it is sometimes found in old music for the harpsichord. But in writing for voices, or for instruments of limited compass, a section of the eleven-lined stave is selected, covering as nearly as possible the range of the voice or instrument, and the place of the C clef, which always fixes the position of middle C, shows what section has been selected.*

As long as the correct pronunciation of the words marked all the rhythm necessary for plain chant, notation by neumæ written on

---

* The treble, called also violin or G clef, and the bass, or F clef, are used only with the upper or lower group of five lines; because then the middle C does not form part of the stave. For any other group of lines the C clef must be used.

alternate lines and spaces was sufficiently exact. But for the notation of rhythmic melody (measured chant) it was necessary to express the relative duration, as well as the actual pitch, of the notes. The first to solve this problem was Franco of Cologne, who in the eleventh century invented the 'large,' the 'long,' the 'breve' and the 'semibreve,' which

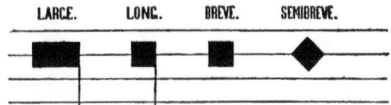

corresponds to our whole note. The 'minim,' the 'crotchet,' the 'quaver' and 'semiquaver' —terms still used in England for half, quarter, eighth and sixteenth notes—were invented several centuries later, and were for a long time used only for embellishments. The minim—corresponding to our half-note—was called minim (least) because it was supposed that a note representing a smaller value would never be required.

The notes of measured chant were at first entirely black, afterward their value was

sometimes altered by color; but in the fourteenth century both black and colored forms

were superseded by hollow, white notes with square, or diamond-shaped, heads.

Here is a table of comparative values of these notes. In this table each note is represented as equal to two of the next lower in value; but this was not always the case. At first the rhythm was always triple, and each note was equal to three of the next smaller. This triple rhythm was called perfect,* and was denoted in the time signature by a circle, preceded by groups of rests showing the proportion between the notes employed. When, somewhat later, duple, or quadruple,

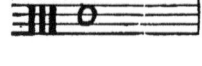

---

* The mediæval significance of the number three, derived from the Blessed Trinity.

time was introduced, it was called imperfect, and was represented in the time signature by a half-circle—from which is derived our sign for common, or quadruple, time. Still later, the groups of rests were replaced by figures, and so originated the modern time signatures.

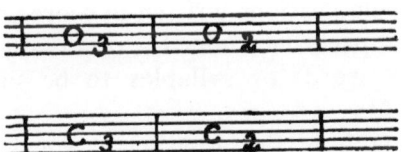

In measured chant—which was so called to distinguish it from plain chant, in which all

the notes were of the same length—there were no bars, the rhythm being shown by the value of the notes. But as this value was affected by the order in which the notes followed one another, a dot (or hook) was sometimes introduced to separate the rhythmic periods.

This dot, which corresponded to the modern bar, was called the point of division. There were also the point of perfection (which preserved the value of a note), the point of alteration (which lessened its value), and the point of addition, or augmentation, which was identical with our modern dot; adding one-half to the value of the note after which it was placed.

The bar was first used, about the close of the sixteenth century, to facilitate the reading of compositions written in score—that is, with the parts one under the other—by marking the words or syllables to be sung together.*

Although in the notation of vocal music letters were early superseded by neumæ and mensural notes, yet for instrumental music—particularly for organ and lute—they were used down even into the seventeenth century. This kind of notation, which was called tablature, had above the letters that indicated the pitch signs denoting the value of the notes; a point for the breve, a stroke for the

---

* The first note of the measure is not accented because it comes immediately after the bar, but the bar is placed before the note which naturally receives the accent; which explains why a composition does not always begin with a full measure.

semibreve, a little tail, or streamer, for the minima and two for the semiminima, and corresponding signs for the rests.

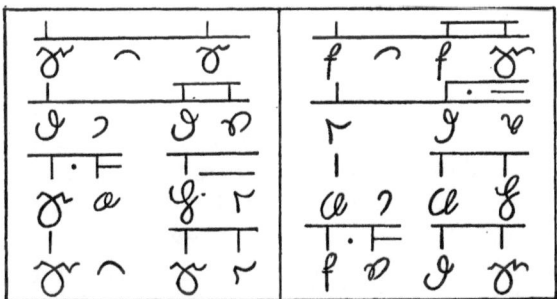

From this notation the organist was expected to read. The tablature for the lute had also numbers indicating the positions, or fingering.

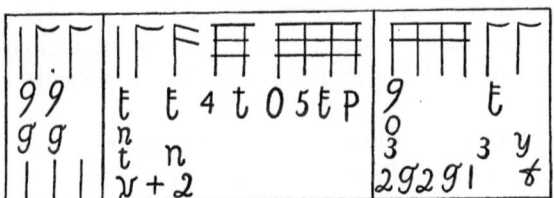

From this tablature-notation have been borrowed, probably, the forms for our smaller notes and rests, as well as the method of grouping the former by common strokes.

For many centuries music—that is, learned, scientific music—was entirely under the control of the Church and strictly regulated by ecclesiastical authority. Doubtless the common people had their own songs and dance tunes, but the learned monks who wrote all the treatises and preserved all the manuscripts did not deem them worthy of record; so for about a thousand years the only music of which we have any real history is church music. We frequently, however, meet with mention of the minstrels who lived at the various courts, or travelled about visiting the great houses and castles and singing ballads and love-songs. These wandering musicians were always welcome everywhere—even in countries with which their own nation might be at war. The Saxon king, Alfred the Great of England, is said to have visited the Danish camp on the eve of a great battle, disguised as a harper.

The troubadours, who first appeared about the close of the eleventh century in the south of France, were generally of higher rank than the minstrels; more than one king was proud to be also a troubadour. Richard Cœur de Lion was one, and the French minstrel, Blondel, who was his teacher, became

Mediæval Music 51

also his friend and companion. We all know the pretty story of how, when Richard on his way home from a crusade was taken captive by the Austrian duke and shut up in prison, no one knew where, Blondel travelled all over Europe, singing his master's favorite songs beneath the windows of each castle and fortress, until at last he heard the king's voice answering with the same song, and could carry back to England the news of where its monarch was imprisoned. Many of the nobles who went to the Holy Land to fight in the crusades were troubadours, and brought back with them Oriental melodies and instruments which had a great influence upon the development of European art.

The troubadours, who were mostly men of rank and station, composed both the poetry and the music to which it was set; but the performance of their compositions, which were chiefly love-songs, was generally intrusted to the professional musicians attached to their retinue, who were called 'jongleurs.'*

These jongleurs, or minstrels, wandered from country to country and from court to court, and sometimes several of them, meet-

---

* From which comes the word juggler.

ing at the same house, would measure their artistic strength in a friendly strife; and in this manner, probably, originated those public contests of song which became such a feature of the thirteenth century.

The 'minnesinger' were a famous brotherhood of German troubadours, who held public competitions for artistic honors. They always sang and accompanied their own compositions, which were not exclusively love-songs, and their art was held in high esteem. The most distinguished of these poet-minstrels were Walther von der Vogelweide, Heinrich von Oefterdingen, Tannhäuser and Wolfram von Eschenbach, and it is one of their contests, the 'Sängerkrieg auf der Wartburg,' which is represented in Wagner's 'Tannhäuser.' The 'meistersinger,' the subject of another of Wagner's operas, endeavored in the fourteenth century to revive the fame of the minnesinger; but they were, as a rule, ignorant and pedantic, and had no lasting influence. They formed themselves into bands, or guilds, for the regulation of contests, and framed elaborate rules for the composition of poetry and music; but they apparently cared more for the rules than for the poetry or music, and did little for the advancement of either art. The most celebrated of the meistersinger was Hans Sachs, of Nuremberg, whom Wagner has immortalized. The minstrels, troubadours and minnesinger played a very important part in the development of the music of the Middle Ages, and from the eleventh to the fourteenth century these musicians exercised a wide influence.

III

The Belgian School

IT was not in France, where the achievements of the troubadours seemed to promise so much—nor in Germany, where the art of the minnesinger was held in such high esteem—nor in England, where music was early cultivated and appreciated—nor in Italy, where the people have such sweet voices and the language almost sings itself, and where in the fourteenth century the art of improvisation was so much admired—but in a little country in the north of Europe that music sustained its first great development. How did it happen that under the cold, gray skies and amid the flat, dull landscape of the Netherlands the art of music flourished more than in sunny France or beauty-loving Italy? It was because the Low Countries were at this time prosperous and powerful, under a liberal government and at peace with all the earth. France was distracted by war with England and plots and insurrections at home. In Germany the struggle between pope and emperor kept the land in a continual turmoil. In England, besides the war with France, there was bloody internal strife; and in Italy—whose commerce surpassed that of Holland—whose merchants lived in princely luxury—where the arts of painting and architecture flourished — the cities, instead of uniting like the cities of the Netherlands in peaceful festivals which stimulated the development of musical art, were constantly involved in sanguinary feuds; and even in individual families jealousy and hatred were handed down from generation to generation. So in all Europe the only peaceful corner for the art of music was in the Netherlands.

The musical development of the Netherlands was exclusively in the direction of counterpoint. For many centuries music consisted of melody only. Harmonic combinations were known to the Greeks, though they apparently did not use them in performance, and very early writers mention symphony and diaphony—meaning, probably, consonant and dissonant intervals. But the earliest departure from strictly unisonal singing seems to have been in the tenth century, when Hucbaldus, the Flemish monk who experimented with the stave, accompanied various melodies with a part forming consecutive fifths or fourths—progressions unbearably harsh to

or

modern ears *—which crude accompaniment was called 'organum.'

This was succeeded by a more elaborate system called 'discantus,' which was the transition from organum to counterpoint. In discant other intervals than fifths and fourths were permitted, and the voices moved sometimes in opposite directions, instead of al-

---

* The unpleasant effect of consecutive fifths seems to be due to their suggestion of different tonalities and abrupt passage from one to another. As in the Middle Ages the fifth represented merely a perfect consonance—modern tonalities being as yet unrecognized—the succession of such intervals was probably not disagreeable to mediæval ears.

The Belgian School

ways parallel; so that the harshness of the organum was generally avoided.*

Singers were taught to improvise the discant, and of this music we have, naturally, little or no record. The only music that has been preserved unchanged from the first thousand years of the Christian Church is the plain-song, or melody of the Gregorian tones or chants. "This," says Ambros, "is the true rock of Peter, around which ebbed and flowed the vanishing waves of the improvised discant."

But discant, although a great improvement upon organum, was a mere succession of consonant intervals, and developed into real counterpoint only as the importance of dissonances became more fully recognized. Counterpoint is the art of combining melodies. Some old chant or familiar tune was taken as a foundation, spaced off in very long notes and given to the tenor voice. To this, which was called the 'canto fermo,' were added, both above and below, more or less

---

* Because the discant was frequently higher in pitch than the melody to which it was added, the name was later applied to the soprano part, or the instrument playing that part, and so came to mean an air or melody.

elaborate melodies for the other voices—each melody independent and complete in itself. As the notes were in those days called points, the added melody was called the counterpoint—point against point. If the foundation tune was not long enough for the words it was repeated — sometimes backward, for variety—with new counterpoint each time. Modern music is a melody with an accompaniment built upon chords; but contrapuntal music is formed of distinct and independent melodies which are sung or played together. Modern music is regarded, as it were, perpendicularly; the melody, and below, or sometimes above it, the harmony—chords, or arpeggios, or figures of any sort which form the accompaniment. Contrapuntal music must be regarded horizontally; the melody upon which the composition is based—the canto fermo — and other melodies, either above or below it, which, though they may when combined form successions of chords, are yet distinct and independent melodies.

In early days vocal music was the only important branch of the art. The instruments were not capable of playing anything but the simplest melodies. The voices usually sang without accompaniment, or, if instruments were used, they played just what the voices sang. Doubtless the early musicians, if they had had an instrument like the piano-forte upon which to experiment, would very quickly have discovered chords and all the harmonic figures that are now used in accompaniments. But their instruments were very imperfect, while human voices were just as beautiful as they are to-day; so they composed exclusively for voices, and it was natural that they should think of each voice separately and give to each an independent part.

The early counterpoint was very formal and severe, and the rules for its composition extremely strict. The canto fermo—the melody to which the counterpoint was added—was always arranged in long notes of equal length, and the counterpoint was carefully classified. There were two kinds—plain, or simple, and double. Plain counterpoint might be note against note

two notes against one

three or four notes against one

syncopated

or florid.

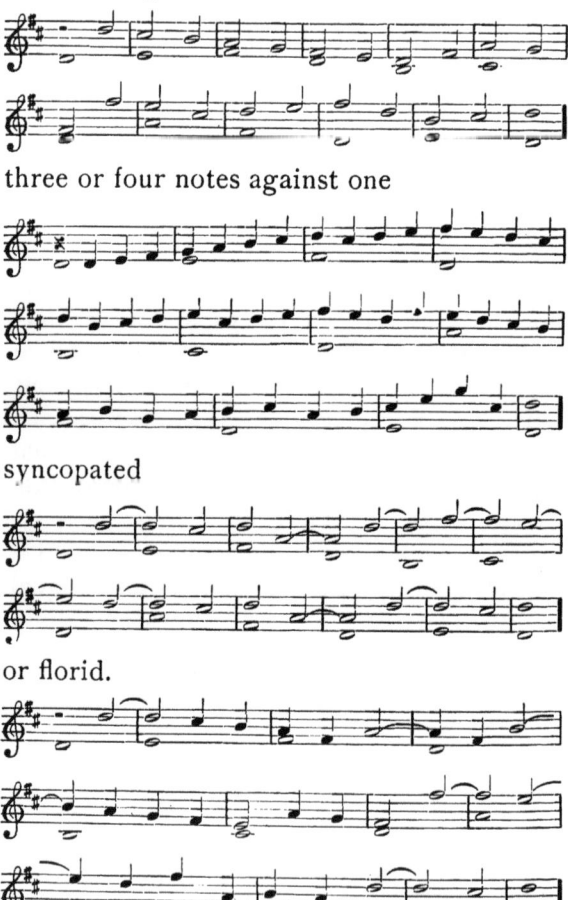

When the parts might be inverted the counterpoint was called double.

Inversion.

These examples are of the very simplest description, only one voice carrying a counterpoint against the canto fermo; but by the addition of two, three, four, six, eight, or even more voices, each with its own melodious counterpoint, the richest and most elaborate musical works might be constructed—as, for instance, the great Italian masses of the sixteenth century.

Although in strict counterpoint, which was essentially vocal, the canto fermo was always in notes of equal length, with the development of instrumental music a freer style was gradually introduced, in which notes of various lengths were permitted in all the parts.

It is in this freer style that the great works, both vocal and instrumental, of the eighteenth century (Bach and Händel) are composed.

The northern musicians who in the fifteenth and sixteenth centuries so elaborated the art of counterpoint are known as the Belgian school. The art did not originate with them —the earliest known polyphonic (contrapuntal) composition is English—but they took the lead of all other nations in its development. One of them, Guillaume Dufay (1380–1430), is said to have invented the canon, which is the strictest kind of musical composition—the part for the first voice being exactly repeated by all the others, beginning at different times.

This canon is brought to a conclusion, and is of the kind called finite; but many canons lead back to the beginning, and thus become perpetual, or infinite.

For such compositions as these it was sufficient to write a single part, appending a rule, or canon, for the entrance of the voices; and from this, which was a very common manner of writing, probably originated the name. These rules, or canons, were often riddles or puns which the singer was expected to guess. By the canon 'Crescit in duplo' the composer indicated that the following voice should double the value of the notes. By the canon 'Qui se exaltat humiliabitur' the second voice was directed to rise when the first descended and fall when it ascended, etc. The Belgian musicians wrote canons in the most fantastic ways. Some could be sung equally well with the book upside down, or backward. Here is one of the kind called 'cancrizans'—crablike —because of its retrograde motion.

It seems to have been the aim of these old contrapuntists to produce canons which are almost incomprehensible. They wrote them in circles and triangles and other shapes, or even simply indicated them by monograms and symbols, concealing in an enigma the key to the solution.

These curious old compositions seem to us rather trivial, though they must have cost their composers much labor and pains, and they have no trace whatever of beauty — the composers caring only for the correct ordering of the intervals—but it was really by means of such experiments that the early musicians discovered the relations of tones and all the possibilities of combination which their successors turned to such good account. It was this severe training in the strict school of dry and artificial counterpoint that prepared the way for the glorious development of the sixteenth century.

One of the most noted of the Belgian musicians was Josquin des Prés (1440-1521), of whom Luther said that he "was master of notes while others were mastered by them." The historian Ambros says that he is the first composer whose works create an impression of genius. Des Prés certainly seems to have had a new revelation concerning music. He says: "It is not enough that the contrapuntal voices shall appear in well-sounding and dignified combinations—music hath also a speech and capacity for the expression of the pain and pleasure of the human breast." Des Prés is the first composer whose works have survived in sufficient quantity to fairly represent his achievements—the invention of printing music by movable types,* which so stimulated publication, dating from his day. Before that time music had been printed only in coarse wood-cuts.

All really fine copies of musical works were made with pen and brush—generally in characters so large and distinct that the whole choir could sing from one enormous folio opened before it on a reading-desk. Such richly illuminated volumes in costly bindings are to-day counted among the greatest treasures of cathedrals and monasteries.

---

*Ottaviano dei Petrucci, about 1500.

ILLUMINATED MANUSCRIPT (FIFTEENTH CENTURY) IN THE IMPERIAL LIBRARY, VIENNA.

The Belgian School

But the greatest of the Belgian musicians was Orlando Lassus (1520–95), who spent most of his life as director of the ducal chapel in Munich, where honors and riches were showered upon him. He was called the 'Prince of Music,' received letters of nobility from the emperor, and from the pope the coveted order of the Golden Spur. Lassus, who excelled in both sacred and secular music, produced an immense number of works (about two thousand), and his fame, even during his lifetime, was widespread. He was undoubtedly the greatest composer of the sixteenth century, with the single exception of his illustrious contemporary, Palestrina.

IV

Music in Italy

THE Italians of the fourteenth and fifteenth centuries had a lively appreciation of music and much natural talent, and the art of improvisation, which they held in the highest esteem, was widely practised. But this kind of emotional song, though it did much for the development of melody, could not lead to the higher art which is founded upon tones in combination—harmony—and the impulse toward this higher art was first given in Italy by the Netherlanders. In the fifteenth century Dutch singers, composers, teachers and theoreticians held the first positions all over Italy, and exerted a decisive influence upon the development of music in that country.

When, about the beginning of the fourteenth century, Pope Clement V. transferred the papal chair to Avignon, the papal choir remained in Rome, and in the new capital a new choir was formed consisting largely of Flemish singers, who, as had been their custom, added discant and vocal ornaments to the plain-song of the church service. Though efforts were made (notably by Pope John XXII.) to purify the Gregorian chant from these additions, under later pontiffs the papal court at Avignon became the seat of such luxury and magnificence that vocal display in the service was encouraged rather than repressed. When, toward the close of the century, Gregory IX. finally returned to Rome, the Avignon choir accompanied him and was amalgamated with the Roman chapel; and with the admission of the Netherlanders and their compositions into the papal choir was decided their predominant influence in Italy.

Music, by this time, had ceased to be the monopoly of the Church, and the Netherlanders worked in all directions for its development. One of them, Adrian Willaert (1490–1563), chapelmaster at St. Mark's in Venice, is thought to have been the inventor of the madrigal, which is an unaccompanied song for several voices in the polyphonic (contrapuntal) style, and in the sixteenth century represented the highest form of secular, as the mass the highest form of sacred, music. The madrigal flourished chiefly in Italy and in England. In the latter country during the reign of Queen Elizabeth it became extremely popular in aristocratic circles, and not to be able to sing a part at sight was counted as a lack of culture and education. The madrigals of the sixteenth and seventeenth centuries are probably the best music that England has produced.

In a few generations the teachings and influence of northern musicians in Italy had developed a school of native composers, who first rivalled and then outshone the former, and of which the culminating glory was Giovanni da Palestrina (1528-94), who died just as the dawn of the monodic style—the *new* music, as it was called—began to glow above the horizon.*

---

* In polyphonic (contrapuntal) music all the parts are of equal importance and all equally melodious, while in monodic (homophonic) music the chief melody is given to one prominent part or voice, to which all the others are subordinated to form an accompaniment. The choruses of Händel's 'Messiah' are splendid examples of polyphony, while the solos " He shall feed his flock," and " I know that my Redeemer liveth," are homophonic or monodic.

Palestrina's name is most prominently associated with the attempted reformation of ecclesiastical music by the celebrated Council of Trent. Complaints against the abuse of contrapuntal elaborations in the music of the church service had become so loud that in 1562 the council seriously contemplated the prohibition of figural (contrapuntal) music altogether, and the restoration in its place of the ancient, simple Gregorian chant. It was not the reform of the art of music, however, at which the council aimed, but the reform of the church ritual. The Gregorian chants were designed to add to the impressiveness of this ritual—the words being the principal thing, the music of value only as it enhanced their importance. But although the masses and motets were generally founded upon these old chants, they were so obscured by the elaborate counterpoint of the composers and the ornaments added by the singers as to be quite unrecognizable, and a few syllables were made the occasion for such a vast number of notes as to become absolutely unintelligible. Moreover, the masses and motets were often founded upon secular melodies, which, though they in like manner disappeared beneath the complications of the counterpoint, yet gave their names to the compositions and were often actually sung to the words with which they were habitually associated; so that with the most solemn phrases of the mass were mingled the refrains of indecorous songs.

It would, however, be unjust to infer that the Netherlanders, to whom the introduction of secular songs as canti fermi for sacred compositions is due, had any thought of profanation or indecorum. They were used to the intermingling of every-day life with sacred art—their own portraits appear in altar-pieces with saints and angels—apostles and martyrs are depicted with the most realistic Dutch surroundings—and it seemed to them natural enough that their popular songs should be used in the service of the Church. In Rome, where the custom would, perhaps, not have originated, the fame of the Netherland musicians and the real merit of their compositions secured for them admittance into the papal chapel and acceptance as models by the Italian composers.

In the council the most zealous of the reformers advocated the restriction of music in the church service to the ancient, Gregorian plain-chant; but, fortunately, there were also true music-lovers and cultivated amateurs, and the decree was finally modified to a warning against the abuse of contrapuntal devices and the introduction of words foreign to the prescribed text, and to the exclusion of masses founded upon secular melodies. As to what kind of contrapuntal music would not interfere with the clear understanding of the words, it was resolved to make a practical test; and Palestrina, whose reputation was already great, was invited to compose a work which should prove that artistic music could be made to heighten, rather than lessen, the effect of the words. With what zeal and devotion he undertook the task is shown by the motto he chose—" Lord, illumine mine eyes "—and by the fact that, in place of one, he wrote three masses; the last of which, dedicated to Pope Marcellus and known as the 'Missa Papæ Marcelli,' is universally recognized as the greatest musical composition of the sixteenth century. Its performance before a commission of cardinals was so convincing, that figural music was tacitly, if not formally, received into ecclesiastical favor and accorded the protection which was necessary to insure the future development of the art.

The pope's verdict upon Palestrina's mass has become celebrated. "These," said he, "are the harmonies of the new song which the Apostle John heard out of the heavenly Jerusalem, and of which an earthly John (Giovanni) in an earthly Jerusalem gives us a foretaste."

V

Evolution of the Modern Scale

AS long as music consisted of melody only, the ecclesiastical modes, or scales, answered every purpose. It is a mistake to consider the modern major and minor forms as the standard scales. They are only the standard scales of the musical development of the last three centuries in western Europe. A composer may use any scale that his hearers can understand, and are willing to accept. The Arabian scale comprises seventeen degrees to the octave—our step of a whole tone being divided into three—and is perfectly comprehensible and acceptable to ears which are familiar with it. In primitive music the most common scale is the pentatonic, consisting of but five degrees and cor-

responding exactly to the modern major scale with the fourth and seventh omitted. The melodies of the American Indians and negroes are largely constructed upon this scale,

NEGRO MELODY (PENTATONIC).

as are also those of many Asiatic nations.

CHINESE MELODY (PENTATONIC).

This pentatonic scale is characteristic of Scotch music also. The familiar old tune of 'Bonnie Doon' is a pentatonic melody.

Evolution of the Modern Scale

A characteristic Hungarian scale has two augmented seconds, * and still other scales are used in other countries.

Since the sixteenth century, music has been composed mostly in the modern major and minor scales, or keys, but many melodies with which we are quite familiar are in scales exactly corresponding to the ancient ecclesiastical modes. The Scotch and Irish tunes that sound so weird and strange are generally constructed upon scales in which, according to the standard of the modern scale, the semitones are displaced. This beautiful old Irish melody is in a scale having semitones between the second and third, and sixth and seventh degrees.

* Three half-tones or steps.

Here is another, in a scale which has semitones between the second and third, and fifth and sixth degrees.

Evolution of the Modern Scale

Modern composers sometimes use these old scales to produce special effects. The ballad of the 'King of Thule' in Gounod's 'Faust' is an example.

If it were in the modern scale of A minor, the G in the second measure would be made sharp. In one of Beethoven's later quartets is a movement which he entitles 'Song of Thanksgiving in the *Lydian Mode*, offered to the Almighty by a Convalescent;' * and many other examples might be quoted to illustrate the occasional use of ancient scales by modern composers.

Until about the beginning of the seventeenth century all musical compositions were in the ecclesiastical modes, or scales. These may be pretty well represented on the white keys of the piano-forte key-board, each scale beginning with a different letter and the semitones, or half-steps, falling between different degrees—thus giving to each a distinctive character; whereas our modern major or

---

* It was the Lydian mode, or scale, which mediæval writers called Modus Laetus, the Joyful Mode—most appropriate for a convalescent.

minor scales are virtually the same scale transposed higher or lower—the sharps and flats being used to bring the semitones always between the same relative degrees.

A characteristic of all modern scales is the leading note—that on the seventh degree—which is always a semitone below the keynote, or tonic, into which it seems naturally to lead. This note is essential to the modern system of harmony. But in most of the ecclesiastical scales the note immediately below the tonic was separated from it by the interval of a whole tone, and a few of the simplest chord progressions transposed into one of them will show how impossible they were for harmonic combinations.

It was early discovered that a really well-sounding counterpoint, or accompanying melody to a canto fermo, could not be written without occasionally introducing accidentals to change the position of the semitones. As the voices combined to form chords it was found that to make them agreeable to the ear the seventh note of the scale must be a semitone, or half-step, below the tonic, or key-note; and as the appreciation of harmonic relations became more and more definite, the raising of this seventh by an accidental became more and more common. Zarlino, the most progressive theoretician of the sixteenth century, says: " Nature herself demands the leading note—even the peasants who know nothing of the art of music sound it naturally as the proper interval." But among educated musicians there long existed a prejudice against the use of these accidentals, and in the canto fermo—the plain-song of the Church—they were expressly forbidden by ecclesiastical authority; so they seldom appeared in writing, but the choristers were taught to introduce them correctly at sight, and trained singers so resented the introduction of what they considered an unnecessary accidental that they called it 'signum asininum '—an ass's mark.*

By the middle of the seventeenth century the ecclesiastical scales had become so altered by the introduction of these accidentals that their essential characteristics had entirely disappeared, and they were finally fused into the two forms of the Ionian (C major) and Æolian (which, with the raised seventh, is the modern scale of A minor). For a long time the scale of C major was called the Ionian and the scale of A minor the Æolian —the other scales, in which the same succession of whole and half-steps was obtained by the use of flats and sharps, being regarded as transpositions of these two.

---

* Even now, in the modern minor scale the raising of the seventh is effected by an accidental, instead of being indicated in the signature, as it logically should be.

VI

The Opera

MODERN music dates from the birth of Italian opera in the year 1600. The union of music with dramatic poetry to heighten the emotional effect of the words existed, however, centuries before that date. It seems to be established almost beyond a doubt that the Greek drama, which probably originated in the religious pantomimic dances that were always accompanied by song, was intoned, or chanted, and the choruses sung to the best music of their time. Unfortunately, we have no means of knowing what this music was, for no manuscripts of Greek music-dramas have been preserved, and for many centuries both music and drama were alike forgotten. But after the night of the dark ages and the twilight of the Middle Ages came the dawn of the Renaissance, in which the admiration for everything classical became a predominating influence in the development of all the arts; and modern opera was the result of an effort on the part of some enthusiastic Italians to revive the style of musical declamation which they supposed had been used by the Greek dramatists.

Toward the close of the sixteenth century a little circle of classical scholars and cultured amateurs met frequently at the house of Giovanni Bardi, in Florence, to discuss, from an intellectual stand-point, the revival of the classic drama—that is, a drama in which the expression and effect of the poetry are heightened and intensified by union with music. Among them were also two or three musicians who endeavored to put their theories into practice. But the musical art of the sixteenth century, which consisted exclusively of the artificial devices and puzzling intricacies of counterpoint, was quite incapable of expressing anything like dramatic emotion; so they concentrated their efforts upon the invention of a new style, resembling, as they fondly hoped, the musical declamation of the ancient Greeks. This new style of music was called homophonic, or monodic, in contradistinction to polyphonic.

It is indispensable to have a clear idea of the difference between the two. Polyphonic music is constructed by interweaving melodies—" its harmonies are not aim, but result." Although some one melody is taken as the foundation of a polyphonic composition, this melody is generally so obscured by the addition of others as to become almost unrecognizable, and has absolutely no influence as to character or rhythm upon the composition as a whole. Homophonic, monodic music, on the contrary, seeks to intensify the character of the melody by an accompaniment of subordinate harmonies, so that the composition as a whole is dominated by the melody. Contrapuntal (polyphonic) music is strictly impersonal in its nature—though each part is in itself complete all are equally subordinate to the whole; while in music intended to arouse personal emotion, that is, dramatic music, individualism predominates — everything else being subordinated to one prominent melodic idea.

Dramatic performances associated with music were by no means unknown in the sixteenth century. In Italy there were classical allegories, in England and France masques and ballets, with songs, choruses, dance tunes and instrumental interludes. But in these pieces the dialogue was spoken, and the music merely interpolated to increase the pleasing effect of the whole. Toward the close of the century one very curious and interesting attempt was made to illustrate the drama by high class, polyphonic music. In this work, which the composer, Orazio Vecchi (1551–1605), calls a "harmonious comedy," the story is told in a series of madrigals for five voices in the true polyphonic style. There is no attempt at instrumental accompaniment, but the characters who appear upon the stage are supported by the other voices behind the scenes; these voices corresponding in a measure to the modern orchestra.

But this kind of music was quite incompetent to illustrate dramatic poetry. The polyphonic style, so perfect an exponent of religious sentiment, failed utterly to express human stress and passion, and the founders of the Florentine school of opera started out in quite a different direction. It was upon æsthetic grounds, however, not musical, that the inventors of the lyric drama rejected polyphony. As music they acknowledged the value of the older compositions, but dramatic expression demanded another style. Their first invention was the cantata—a musical recitation of a short story in verse by a single person accompanied by a single instrument —and some of these compositions were published under the title of 'The New Music.'

These cantatas, which were quite different from the modern compositions known by the same name, consisted exclusively of recitative. The aim of the composers was not to make tunes, but to intensify the expression of the words by declaiming them to musical sounds. Rhythmic and melodious phrases were purposely avoided, as being absolutely detrimental to the desired effect. "The new music," says a contemporary writer (Giovanni Battista Doni), "is a kind of melody so sung by a single voice that the words are well understood, with little dwelling upon single tones; so that the song approaches somewhat to ordinary speech, but is more expressive."

Simple melody, with little or no accompaniment, was not heard for the first time in Florence at the close of the sixteenth century. It had existed in popular song and dance tunes ages before the birth of those enthusiasts who then and there introduced it to the amateurs of the city. But it had been accepted by educated musicians only as the canto fermo on which to build their great polyphonic compositions, and even the inventors of the lyric drama, who repudiated polyphony, avoided formal tunes and aimed solely at the exact rhetorical rendering of the words by what is called recitative.

In 1597 the first opera, 'Dafne,' by Jacopo Peri, was privately performed at the Palazzo Corsi in Florence. This work, which has, unfortunately, been lost, was called 'Dramma per la Musica,' and it was not till half a century later that the word opera was applied to such compositions. The success of Peri's first effort was so decided that he was invited to provide a similar work for the festivities attending the marriage of King Henry IV. of France with Maria de' Medici, and in the year 1600 was produced in Florence his famous 'Euridice'—the first Italian opera ever performed in public. Seven years later was brought out in Mantua, on the occasion of another great marriage, an opera by Claudio Monteverde (1566–1650), a composer whose innovations in the use of chords had already attracted much attention. Monteverde's chief innovations were in the use of the imperfect, or diminished, triad and the unprepared dissonances of the chords of the seventh and ninth.

Triads are of three kinds: major, minor, and imperfect, or diminished, and the use

of the diminished triad was permitted only under restrictions by the older school. Triads are the only chords which are consonances—that is, which are in themselves satisfactory to the ear and do not demand to be followed by other harmonies—and they are the basis of all other chords, which are formed from them by the addition of superimposed thirds.

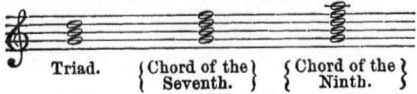

In these chords the seventh and ninth are dissonances and require resolution—that is, to be followed by their nearest related triads.

A dissonance is said to be prepared when the dissonant tone appears first as a consonance in the immediately preceding chord.

Prepara-   Disso-   Resolution.   nance.   tion.

In later times the use of unprepared dissonances has become so common that a composer may even *begin* with a chord of the seventh or ninth without exciting remark; but in Monteverde's day these harmonies aroused as much opposition and controversy as any of Wagner's have done in more recent years. Monteverde's genius insured the success of the new style. He not only emancipated the dissonances, making them a principal means of passionate expression, but not, like the Florentines, content merely to illustrate the text word by word with appropriate melody, he aimed also at dramatic characterization by the orchestra, which he largely increased.

At first there were no public opera-houses—the musical drama was an entertainment reserved for the courts of princes and made the occasion for fabulous display on occasions of public festivity—but in 1637 the first opera-house was opened in Venice, and the passion for musical representations soon spread throughout Italy. In Venice, Cavalli (1599-1676), a pupil of Monteverde, first introduced fluent, rhythmic melody—what we call tune—into the opera, and with him begins a departure from the ideal of the Florentines. Their first principle was that the music should be only a means of intensifying the expression of the poetry. They had no thought of making tunes—melodies which might be separated from the text and played on an instrument with pleasing effect. The recitatives which they composed are absolutely meaningless without the words. But with Cavalli the music begins to assert an independence that rapidly developed into a mastery, and before long dominated the whole structure of the opera to the destruction of all dramatic effect.

An immense number of operas was produced during the seventeenth century; slight works, often little more than mere excuses for the display of gorgeous costumes and the art of the stage machinist. The Italians had long been accustomed to displays of great magnificence upon occasions of public great magnificence upon occasions of public festival, and a splendid setting soon became indispensable to the success of a musical drama.

Alessandro Scarlatti (1659-1725), the father of the famous harpsichord player, was by far the best composer of this period. He developed and fixed the form of the aria by the addition of a second part followed by that repetition of the first part known as the Da Capo—which monotonous form predominated in the opera for more than a century. Scarlatti, who was thoroughly trained in the science of composition, did much for the development of instrumental music, also; his accompaniments being far superior to those of any of his predecessors. The earlier dramatic composers thought the study of counterpoint unnecessary, and were content to accompany their recitatives with only a few simple chords; but Scarlatti brought all the resources of musical art to the support of the new style, and thus placed modern music upon a secure foundation.

The 'Euridici' of Peri, performed at Florence in the year 1600, excited an extraordinary amount of attention throughout the musical world, and everywhere composers were fired with ambition to emulate its success. England in the seventeenth century produced her greatest native composer, Henry Purcell (1658-95), whose operas are quite equal to those of his contemporaries. He, unfortunately, died too young to found a school and has had no worthy successor. As early as 1627, 'Dafne,' translated into German, and set to music by Heinrich Schütz (1585-1672), was performed at Torgau, but the real foundations of German opera were laid at Hamburg by Reinhard Keiser (1673-1739), who has the honor of being the first of that great German school to which the world is indebted for its finest dramatic composers. In France the first opera performed in public was 'Pomone' (1669), by Cambert and Perrin, but the true founder of French opera was Giovanni Battista Lulli (1633-87), an Italian, brought as a child to France, and early taken into favor by the king for his skill in composing the ballets in which the youthful monarch, who was passionately fond of dancing, himself took part. Lulli invented a style of recitative so perfectly adapted to illustrate the best French dramatic poetry that it became the foundation of the French grand opera.*

---

* In the French grand opera every word is sung to orchestral accompaniment. In the opéra comique, on the contrary, the dialogue is spoken.

He was also the inventor of the overture. The early Italian operas were preceded only by a very brief introduction, called sinfonia. Even Monteverde, with whom the orchestra becomes of greatly increased importance, introduces 'Orfeo' with only a short prelude of nine measures twice repeated. But Lulli's overture consisted of a slow introduction followed by an allegro and ending with a dance movement—a form which became extremely popular, and long served as a model for composers.

Lulli's greatest follower was Jean Philippe Rameau (1683-1764), who is better known to-day as theorist than as musician. In his celebrated treatise on harmony he shows for the first time the derivation of chords from roots, or fundamental basses, and, also for the first time, advances the theory, since quite generally accepted, that all chords are formed by the addition of superimposed thirds to the triad. The bass of a musical composition is its lowest part; but as chords may be inverted, or rearranged, the lowest tone is not always that which would be the lowest in the original form, or first position, of the chord. That tone, although transferred to an upper part, is still its root, or fundamental bass. Before harmony was reduced to a science, each chord was considered as a distinct and individual combination. Modern harmonists regard chords as belonging to groups, or families, related through their roots, or fundamental basses, and classify them accordingly.

Rameau's operas are chiefly remembered in connection with the 'guerre des bouffons.' The 'opera buffa' originated in the intermezzi, or interludes, which in very early times it was customary to present between the acts of a serious drama. The old Roman comedies had their satires, the mysteries and miracle plays of the Middle Ages hymns and carols sung between the acts, and early Italian plays were almost always relieved by intermezzi. At first these consisted merely of madrigals, or canzonette, but gradually the intermezzi came to embody a distinct little story of their own, having no connection whatever with that of the principal drama; and finally they became so popular that they were given entire as separate pieces. One of the most celebrated of these intermezzi, 'La Serva Padrona,' of Pergolesi—that brilliant young Italian, the flame of whose genius was scarcely lighted before it was extinguished by death—was the occasion of the 'guerre des bouffons' which split the Parisian public into partisans of French and Italian music, enlisting in support of the latter the genius of Rousseau, and arousing an excitement surpassed only by the Gluck and Piccini feud a few years later.

By the middle of the eighteenth century the lyric drama had become a favorite, though always aristocratic, entertainment in all the principal cities of Europe. Modern music was firmly established, and already highly developed.*

But the great development of music, and especially of extreme virtuosity among singers, had destroyed the balance between music and poetry in the opera. The drama had become of little importance save as affording opportunities for musical display, and the singer ruled both poet and composer. In the

---

* However, the very best of the operas which the earlier composers turned out by the dozen, or even by the hundred, was a very slight affair compared to anything that we should consider worthy of the name. A few airs, the elaboration and embellishment of which were entrusted to the singers, connected by recitatives with the simplest of accompaniments, a figured bass to be filled out with chords by the harpsichord player, and parts for strings and a few wind instruments were all that was required of the composer.

earliest Italian operas the characters were divided between men and women; but in the time of Cavalli the artificial male sopranists began to usurp the rôles of the latter, and after the pope forbade the appearance of women upon the Roman stage the soprano and contralto parts were sung almost entirely by these artificial voices. Even in those operas in which women sang the female rôles the artificial sopranos and contraltos monopolized all the principal airs, compelling the composer to minister to their vanity without any regard to the development of the drama; and as great singers became numerous the opera degenerated into a mere collection of arias with a pretence of connection by a thread of recitative. These arias, though differing as to the character of the music, were all alike constructed upon the same plan—the first and second parts followed by the inevitable Da Capo. Some of them contain most amazingly difficult passages, composed especially for those great vocalists whose art apparently consisted in the perfect mechanical delivery of brilliant passages and elaborate embellishments. The famous singing master, Niccolo Porpora, is said to have spent five years training his pupil, the celebrated sopranist Caffarelli, in the execution of one page of transcendently difficult exercises, and then dismissed him, saying : " I have nothing more to teach you—you are the greatest singer in Europe."

It is not as music that the aria has been condemned by critics and reformers. Some arias will always delight the most cultured and critical hearers. But when in the most dramatic situations the action is suspended while the hero or heroine, or both captivate the audience with elaborate displays of vocalism, and the development of the drama is constantly hindered by the music which was intended to illustrate it, there is room for just criticism.

At the climax of its degeneracy, when the drama was completely dominated by the music and the composer ruled by the singer, upon whom the success of his work in no small degree depended, appeared the first reformer of these abuses, Christoph Willibald Gluck (1714–87). Gluck, who in his early days had himself composed successfully in the Italian style, becoming convinced that it was based upon wrong principles, set to work deliberately and conscientiously to effect a reform. In his celebrated dedication of ' Alceste' he says: "I endeavored to reduce music to its proper function—that of seconding poetry by enforcing the expression of the sentiment and the interest of the situation without interrupting the action or weakening it by superfluous ornament. My object was to put an end to all those abuses which had crept into Italian opera through the mistaken vanity of singers and the unwise compliance of composers, and against which good taste and good sense have long protested in vain."

The first tangible embodiment of these ideas was 'Orpheus,' a work which, produced first in Vienna, soon made Gluck's name known all over Europe. But his greatest success was in Paris under the patronage and protection of his former pupil, the dauphiness Marie Antoinette. On the French stage dramatic propriety had never been entirely sacrificed to musical effect, and audiences accustomed to the fine declamation of Lulli and Rameau were well prepared to comprehend the æsthetic principles upon which Gluck's reform was based. He at first carried everything before him. 'Iphigenia in Aulis,' 'Orpheus,' and 'Alceste' were produced, and received with great enthusiasm. But such success was certain to excite opposition. Piccini, an excellent musician, although no match for Gluck, was brought from Italy to be its instrument, and court and society alike separated into hostile ranks. Everybody, who was anybody, declared himself either Gluckist or Piccinist, and the wit and eloquence of the day were divided between the opposing factions. Criticism was answered by epigram and satire with abuse, and the excitement aroused is almost incredible. Gluck was reproached with having no melody and making his singers shriek, with his " noisy orchestra " and " harsh harmonies." Write Wagner for Gluck and one can almost fancy one's self a century later. However, 'Iphigenia in Taurus,' which was the most complete embodiment of Gluck's ideas, assured him a victory over all rivals. Those ideas have already been presented in his own words. His ideal was the same as that to which the Florentine founders of the lyric drama sought to give expression in the as yet imperfect medium of the 'new music;' and Gluck showed that the highest development of musical art might be used in the interest of the drama, instead of sacrificing all dramatic effect to gratify the desire of singers and hearers for brilliant display.

While the strife of the Gluckists and Piccinists was at its height, there came to Paris, where he failed to obtain even a hearing, the most remarkable prodigy and precocious musical genius the world has ever seen—Wolfgang Amadeus Mozart (1756–91). This gifted youth, who at the age of fourteen had written a successful opera, was now at twenty-one a master of every form of composition. But the musical world of Paris was so blinded by the excitement of the Gluck and Piccini controversy that it failed to perceive the newly risen star; and Mozart returned to his native land, where, beset by trials and disappointments and always under the pressure of extreme poverty, he lived out his brief existence.

Mozart did much for the development of dramatic music, inspiring the forms of Italian opera with fresh vitality, but he was never a reformer of its abuses. Although he greatly increased the capacity of music for illustrating poetic intention, and far surpassed all his predecessors in his use of the orchestra as a medium of dramatic effect, he made no effort to change the relation of music and drama in the opera. He was too exclusively a musician—interested in the drama only as affording opportunities for his own art. The perfect musical expression of the sentiment of each situation and the genuine touches of true dramatic pathos which will always compel admiration for Mozart's music, are not incompatible with the fact that he did not hesitate to interrupt the action for its introduction. He, "the most absolute of all musicians," would never for a moment have thought of subordinating music to the drama.

The principles formulated by Gluck were followed by Cherubini (1760-1842), whose operas were so much admired by Beethoven, and by Spontini (1784-1851), whose gorgeous dramatic and spectacular productions dominated the great operatic stages of Europe for many years. Both these composers were Italians by birth and training whose genius was developed under the influence of the great German reformer, and whose greatest successes were made in the French capital. But their influence upon French opera was transitory, and it was in Germany that their works met with the most enduring appreciation. Probably the most representative composer of the modern French grand opera is Meyerbeer (1791-1864), to whose admixture of gorgeous spectacular effects and ballet with music which is by no means lacking in truly dramatic moments, its brilliant reputation is largely due.

'Fidelio,' Beethoven's single opera, stands alone, and seems to have had no influence whatever upon the development of this form of art. Beethoven (1770–1827) was pre-eminently an instrumentalist, and beautiful as is the music of 'Fidelio,' it is yet, as has been said, "more like a symphony for voices and orchestra than the musical complement of a dramatic poem."

In the early part of the present century the genius of Rossini (1792–1868) effected a temporary regeneration of Italian opera — his wonderful gift of melody infusing new life into the old forms and captivating all Europe. But the glamour of this wealth of melodious beauty could not long conceal the fact that the poetic foundation was still a mere excuse for the display of brilliant ornamentation and fascinating dance rhythms, and it is only toward the close of the century that we find, at the hands of the venerable maestro Verdi (1813–   ), who is, perhaps, the most remarkable example of artistic progress and development on record—a real regeneration of

Italian art; so real that it seems almost to foreshadow for Italy, the birthplace of opera, the recovery of her ancient position at the head of musical Europe.

The founder of what is known as the German Romantic school of opera was Carl Maria von Weber (1786–1826), a composer whose influence is apparent in even the latest development of German art. The derivation of the word romantic explains its meaning— the mediæval legends and tales of love and chivalry written in the old Romance dialects being called romances. The group of German writers who about the beginning of the present century rescued these old romances from oblivion, came to be known as the Romantic school of literature; and the term was applied also to Weber's operas, all of which are founded upon romantic subjects. The music which illustrates a romantic poem is naturally less restricted by form than that which is called classical—it must express, as freely and directly as possible, the poetic imaginings of the composer; so, when these terms are applied to pure, absolute music, not associated with words, classical music is music composed in the established forms (symphony, sonata, rondo, etc.), while romantic music seeks simply to give the most direct and vivid expression to the thoughts and feelings of the composer. Classical composers are those who have developed accepted musical forms into an adequate medium for the expression of their thoughts. Romantic composers are those who have expressed their ideas in the most direct manner, irrespective of any formal limitations. But since the word classical * means, primarily, of the first rank, when a musician of to-day composes in the regular, established forms, we do not say that his work is classical, but only in the classical style. If time proves that his work is really of the first rank, *classicus*, then it is called classical.

Weber's opera is founded on the 'volkslied' —that form of song which, Ambros says, is in its importance for the European development of music second only to the Gregorian chants. A volkslied is a song of the people. It is a composition without a composer. When the improvised melody of

---

* From the division of the citizens of ancient Rome into ranks or classes according to their incomes, for purposes of taxation. The citizen of the highest rank was called simply *classicus*—of the class—just as we say men of rank, implying of the first rank.—TRENCH.

some primitive singer pleases the hearers, it is naturally remembered and repeated—occasionally with variations which, if they commend themselves to their audience, are accepted as part of the song ; and so, from generation to generation the melody is passed on, and modified by one singer after another until it is finally written down by some collector of volkslieder. A melody which is composed in the style of a volkslied is called 'volksthümlich,' but a true volkslied has no recognized composer. The charm of the volkslied lies in its concise and regular form and its direct expression of popular feeling ; and these qualities Weber embodied in his music.

Weber excelled all of his predecessors in his use of the orchestra as a means of dramatic characterization. Before his time, instruments were used chiefly to support the voices and impart sonority to the general effect, but Weber, with a marvellous comprehension of the capacity of each instrument, uses them to characterize both situations and personages.

Richard Wagner (1813-83) is the most recent reformer of the opera, and his reform is so radical, and apparently so enduring, that all the dramatic music of the last few decades is more or less affected by his ideas. With unwonted generosity nature made him both poet and musician, and his dual genius seems finally to have reached the goal toward which the Florentine enthusiasts of the year 1600 set their faces, and successfully united the sister arts of music and poetry—born twins, but long associated under such unnatural conditions as made them often appear like enemies.

Wagner starts with the assumption that there is no possibility of further development for music except in connection with the drama; that the composer must be inspired by a definite poetic idea, and that the mission of music is to receive this idea and bring it forth again transfigured and sublimated. He himself has told us how unintentionally he became a reformer. He was always his own librettist, and having early decided that mythical and legendary subjects are best for musical treatment, he says that the freedom of mythical types implied the liberation of the music itself. "Therefore," says Wagner, "the nature of the subject could not induce me in sketching my scenes to consider in advance their adaptability to any abstract musical form, the particular kind of musical treatment being necessitated by these scenes themselves. It could not enter my mind to engraft on this *my* musical form, growing as it did out of the nature of the scenes, the traditional forms of operatic music, which could only have marred and interrupted its organic progress. I, therefore, never thought of contemplating on principle and as a deliberate reformer the destruction of the aria, the duet and other operatic forms, but the dropping of these forms followed consistently from the nature of my subjects."

For these musical forms Wagner substitutes the continuous melody which glorifies the poetic text. This melody is upborne by the orchestra, which is no longer merely an accompaniment, but has become one of the most important factors in the exposition of the drama. Wagner's orchestra has been compared to the chorus of Greek tragedy, which sometimes continuing the narrative, sometimes commenting upon it, always heightened the dramatic effect. Liszt says in his essay on 'Lohengrin': "To the orchestra he entrusts the function of revealing to us the soul, the passions, the feelings, even the most transient emotions of his characters. His orchestra becomes the echo, the transparent veil through which we note all their heart-beats. In it we hear the angry cry of hatred, the raving of revenge, the whisperings of love, the ecstasy of adoration."

It is by the use of what are called leading motives that Wagner's orchestra is thus intimately associated with the action of the drama. With every agency concerned in its development is identified a typical musical phrase, that recurs whenever the agency with which it is associated is present, even by suggestion. From these themes Wagner, with an unsurpassed command of the orchestra, weaves a grand symphony, which constantly enforces the action of the drama and intensifies its passion. These leading motives are not stereotyped, but are like living organisms, changing and developing with the characters and situations which they illustrate. Though typical phrases that might be called leading motives are to be found in the works of earlier composers, their marvellous use as a distinct principle in the construction of an orchestral exposition of the drama is entirely original with Wagner.

For the realization of his ideal of the true music-drama Wagner demands the co-operation of all the arts—laying almost as much stress upon scenic effects and the mimetic art as upon the poetry and music, but making each and all subservient to the development of the drama.

In his perception of chord relationships Wagner went far beyond any of his predecessors. It is not a matter for wonder that his daring use of harmonic progressions as yet unrecognized should have repelled conservative musicians and excited harsh criticism. It is difficult for the present generation, which has been brought up on such harmonies, to realize the first effect of these progressions. The same old story is repeated everywhere in human history—the strife of conservatism against progress, the opposition of tradition and aspiration. The conservative element, well called the ballast of human society, has always opposed innovation; and, after all, it is right that what is new should be tested by opposition before being accepted. Nothing really worthy of acceptance has ever been hindered by it longer than was necessary for comprehension and appreciation. Innovating musicians have always been compelled to educate a new generation of hearers, and these in their turn become conservatives. Perhaps there is even now in the world a composer who will use chords in yet more distant relationships, and the present generation may in its old age shake its head in disapproval and point to Wagner as a model of simplicity and clearness.

VII

The Oratorio

FROM very early times dramatic performances have been used to teach moral and religious truth and instruct the people in history and legend. Long before any but priests and a few scholars were able to read for themselves, or, indeed, before there were any books, save a few precious manuscripts, there were the miracle plays and mysteries and moralities which are so often mentioned in mediæval records, and which did more for the instruction of the people in sacred history than could possibly have been accomplished by the mere reading of the Scriptures in the churches. They were a kind of object teaching for a population which was still in the kindergarten department of education. The subjects of the plays were the stories of the Old and New

Testaments, the lives of saints, or allegories intended to teach religion and morality,* and it is from these primitive performances, which were usually associated with music, that the modern oratorio has been developed.

There is no record of when or where the dramatic representation of a sacred story was first attempted. As early as the twelfth century crude performances of scenes from Scripture history were not uncommon, and were recognized by the Church as a valuable means of enforcing her own principles and precepts. But though these performances were often under the supervision of the Church, the majority of them were given by strolling companies, who frequently travelled about in a kind of carriage which could be turned into a theatre. This was usually made ready in the inn courtyard, the open galleries surrounding it being occupied by the spectators, but frequently such movable theatres were set up in the city streets, where an audience was always at hand; and though these mediæval performances may seem to us grotesque, and perhaps irreverent, they assur-

---

* The miracle play in Longfellow's 'Golden Legend' gives a very good idea of one.

edly were not so to either performers or onlookers. Finally, however, they became so corrupted by the introduction of absurd stories and traditions, and of comic and vulgar soliloquies and dialogues, that they were prohibited by the Church; yet there were many who advocated their reformation rather than their absolute discontinuance. San Filippo Neri, who was a friend of Palestrina and a great lover of music, thought very highly of them as a means of instruction, and had them frequently performed in the oratory of his church—whence the performances themselves came to be called oratorios.

The year 1600, which saw the birth of monodic music in the Florence opera, witnessed also the production in Rome of the first real oratorio—'L'Animo e Corpo,' by Emilio del Cavalieri. In this work, which is an allegory and the direct descendant of the moralities that were so popular in Italy in the fourteenth and fifteenth centuries, the same ideas regarding music reform were applied to a moral and religious text. The composer, who had been 'inspector of arts' in Florence, had there heard not only the first opera, but also, probably, the discussions which resulted in the invention of the new style of music;

and the influence of the new ideas is apparent in his work. The directions for its performance included scenery, costumes, acting and even dancing on a regular stage—for at first the oratorio differed from the opera only in the choice of its subjects.

The development of early Italian oratorio corresponded exactly with that of early Italian opera—both being treated by the same composers in very nearly the same manner—and the musical value of both operas and oratorios is exceedingly small, judged by our standard. But as monodic music rapidly developed and great singers became numerous, the oratorio, like the opera, began to degenerate into a mere occasion for vocal display. Although the music of Palestrina and his associates remained the officially recognized style of the papal chapel, the enthusiastic admirers of the new music succeeded in introducing it and its virtuoso effects into the churches, which became almost like concert-halls. Nuns were as renowned for their performances as prima donnas, and a difference between religious and secular music was scarcely dreamed of.

The German composers were never so carried away by the new style of music—the monodic—as to neglect the science of composition, like the Italians, and, moreover, they never forgot the distinction between sacred music and secular. In Germany the development of oratorio was much influenced by the chorale—that form of song from which our modern hymn tune is derived.

We know from the New Testament narrative that it was customary for the Jews to sing hymns. The early Christians carried the custom to Rome, and in all probability the melodies which echoed through the catacombs were the same that had been heard in Jerusalem. But when the Church emerged from her obscurity and began to be housed in stately edifices and her service celebrated with an elaborate and impressive ritual, the congregational singing was superseded by that of trained choirs. However, the people continued to sing hymns, and as early as the fifteenth century collections of these began to be published. For many centuries hymns were sung by all the voices in unison; but after the invention of discant and counterpoint the original tunes were supported and surrounded by accompanying melodies, both below and above. In the hymns of all ancient collections the principal melody is always given to the tenor voice; which, indeed,

The Oratorio 117

received its name because it held or kept the principal part. In early times, when women were not permitted to sing in the church choirs, it was natural that what we now call the tenor voice should lead the singing. At first voices were divided only into low and high —bassus, bass, and medius, tenor—but even when a third and higher part,* the alto,† was added, the tenor still carried the principal melody. But with the Reformation appeared a great number of hymns intended for the general congregation. These were adapted to the favorite melodies of the day, both sacred and secular, and in order that all might sing—men, women, and children—the melody was placed in the upper voice and the construction of the tunes made more regular.

And so, upon the volkslied was founded the chorale, which has had the greatest influence upon the development of German music. It was adopted by composers, as the plain-song melodies had been in Italy, and developed to the utmost by the

---

* Called triplum—from which comes the word treble.

† From altus, high; originally the male voice of the highest pitch—the counter tenor, or falsetto. The word soprano comes from the Italian sovrano—sovereign or chief.

genius of John Sebastian Bach (1685-1750). Bach's greatest compositions in the line of oratorio are his settings of the 'Passion of our Lord.' The history of the passion has always formed part of the service for holy week, and very early the custom was introduced of reciting the words to a kind of chant. But besides being a part of the church service the story of the passion was a perennial theme for the miracle plays and mysteries of the Middle Ages. These were always associated with music, and from these primitive works may be traced the development which culminated in Bach's magnificent 'Passion according to St. Matthew.' In this, the words of the Gospel narrative are combined with dramatic choruses and beautiful chorales, sung, not by the choir alone, but by the choir in harmony and by the whole congregation in unison— just as they are sung today in the German Protestant churches.

But Germany was not the country destined to witness the most splendid development of sacred music. In the great English oratorios which have immortalized his name and fixed themselves in the affections of his adopted countrymen with a hold that is scarcely relaxed even at the present day, Händel (1685-

The Oratorio

1759) developed this form of art to the highest pitch of perfection, and proved himself the greatest of choral composers.

When, before the close of the seventeenth century, oratorio began to separate itself from opera by the elimination of scenery, costume and acting, the choral element, which would have been a hindrance to dramatic action, was lifted into prominence. The Italian composers, who concentrated their efforts upon dramatic recitative, deeming contrapuntal skill unnecessary, did comparatively little for its development; but the Germans, who always respected the art of counterpoint, turned all its ingenious devices to account in the service of oratorio—the choruses of Bach's 'Matthew Passion' and of Händel's 'Messiah' and 'Israel in Egypt' being the finest in the world.

The closing years of the eighteenth century witnessed the production of two delightful oratorios, composed by a man who had so nearly reached the allotted term of human life that we can never cease to wonder at the youthful freshness and springlike beauty with which they are pervaded. These were the 'Creation' and 'Seasons' of Joseph Haydn (1732–1809).

Haydn's choruses cannot, of course, be compared with those of the great genius who has been called the "High Priest of the Sublime," but the fluent grace of his melodies and the charm of his instrumental accompaniments were in his own day quite unsurpassed.

Beethoven's single oratorio, like his single opera, stands apart, and exercised no influence upon the development of this form of art.

The composer of the nineteenth century who has embodied in the most glorious forms the noblest ideal of the true oratorio is Felix Mendelssohn (1809-47). 'St. Paul' and 'Elijah' rank second only to the works of the giants, Bach and Händel.

VIII

Instrumental Music

VOCAL music was already highly developed before instrumental music came into existence. Mediæval art was always the child of the Church, and vocal music had been fostered with especial care. In the papal chapel—the typical choir of the Roman church—no instrument was ever used, not even the organ, and the rich treasure of musical compositions preserved in its archives consists exclusively of vocal works. In the Netherlands the voices were sometimes accompanied by instruments, but for these no separate parts were written; they played just what the voices sang. In the sixteenth century independent instrumental music had hardly made a beginning, though we occasionally meet with mention of some clever organist or lute player who was famed for his improvisations. In mediæval times ordinary instrumentalists, pipers, fiddlers, etc., were ranked as vagabonds and outlaws. As late as the eighteenth century in Germany, where music, aside from the church service, was considered chiefly as an aristocratic addition to the domestic establishments of noblemen and great ecclesiastics, musicians not connected with some such establishment were regarded as little better than tramps and vagrants; and even great composers like Haydn and Mozart were reckoned in the list of domestics with cooks and footmen. In Italy music was from the first held in much higher esteem. The musician was regarded as ennobled by his art, and the nobleman did not think it incompatible with his position to practise it himself as an amateur, though the lute was considered to be the only instrument fit for a gentleman.

Until the sixteenth century instruments were not sufficiently perfected to make a real art of playing possible. The clumsy key-boards of the early organs and the great exertion required to produce the sound, precluded the possibility of performing upon these instruments more than the plain-song melody with single accompanying tones;

and even this often required two players. Clavichord and harpsichord were invented but not perfected. The favorite instrument among cultivated amateurs was the lute, whose clear, silvery tones were much to be preferred to the feeble sounds of the as yet imperfect clavier.* The lute, however, had one very great defect—the difficulty of keeping it in tune. Matheson says that if a lute player lived eighty years he had certainly spent sixty of them in tuning his instrument.

Among bowed instruments the viol held the chief place. The stringed instruments of ancient times were always played by being plucked with the fingers, or with a plectrum, but in manuscripts and architectural sculptures of the twelfth century, and even earlier,

---

*Clavier was the general name for all stringed instruments played by means of a key-board.

124   Music

we find representations of such instruments played with a bow; indicating that the bow was by that time in common use throughout Europe. By reason of the deep curves in its

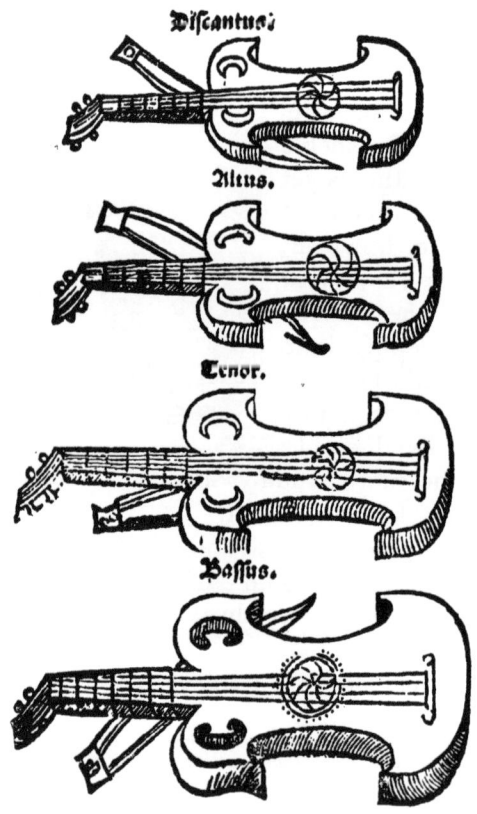

sides, which permitted a freer use of the bow, the viol was a distinct improvement upon any of its predecessors and the direct precursor of the violin. Viols were at first used, as the older instruments had been, merely to support the voice, and were made in different sizes corresponding to the different voices.

A chest of viols—that is, a set of five or six of graduated size and compass—was in the sixteenth century a regular part of the furnishing of a well-appointed house, just as a piano is at the present time. As the madrigals of the sixteenth century were often extremely elaborate and consequently difficult to sing, the parts were frequently accompanied by viols; and sometimes, if there were not voices enough, a voice part was represented by a viol having the same compass. From this it was but a step to playing all the parts with viols, without the voices, and then to composing music professedly intended to be either sung or played.* Sir John Hawkins writes that "when the practice of singing madrigals began to decline, and gentlemen

---

* 'Buone da cantare e suonare' (good to sing and play)—'Apt for voices or viols'—'Convenient for voices or for all kinds of instruments'—are frequently found on the title-pages of early compositions.

and others began to excel in their performances on the viol, the musicians of the time conceived the thought of substituting instrumental music in the place of vocal; and for this purpose some of the most excellent masters of that instrument betook themselves to the framing of compositions called fantazias, which were generally in six parts, answering to the number of viols in a chest, and abounded in fugues, little responsive passages, and all those other elegancies observable in the structure and contrivance of the madrigal."

Early instrumental music is always vocal in character—that is, it is music which could just as well be sung as played. But as instruments of increased compass and capacity were invented, or perfected, instrumental music began to be separated from vocal and to develop a style and character of its own. With the establishment of the monodic style, when the foundation melody, instead of being surrounded by contrapuntal parts of equal importance, was simply supported by an accompaniment of subordinate harmonies, the element of form, which is of such great importance in modern music, begins to appear in instrumental compositions.

In modern terminology the form of a musical work is the arrangement of distinct sections of melody, with such reference to harmonic relationships that the whole impresses the mind as a complete and logical work of art. In vocal compositions the form of the music depends upon the words, but in the construction of purely instrumental works some principle of arrangement and development must be followed.

The association of song and dance early developed definite rhythms and distinct melodic periods—what are commonly called tunes—in popular music, but it was long before these were used by educated musicians except as canti fermi on which to found their counterpoint. The great vocal works of the fifteenth and sixteenth centuries, although they are founded upon distinct melodies, are conspicuously deficient in definite rhythms and phrases; for the tune is so obscured by the accompanying counterpoint that its character and rhythm are utterly lost. Form in its modern sense depends upon defined tonality, and this element, also, is conspicuously absent from the great polyphonic works of the early composers. There could be no development in that direction until the modern scales were accepted and modern principles of harmony fixed; and it was not until the ecclesiastical modes were finally superseded by the major and minor scales, and the relation between chords and distinct keys definitely established, that formal melodies began to be accepted by composers as an important element of high-class music.

The subject of a musical composition is like the text of a sermon—it is the theme upon which the composer discourses—and, like a text, it may consist of a long musical sentence, or a short one, or even a simple phrase; and as a sermon may have several texts, so a musical composition may be developed from several subjects. A complete musical sentence is called a period. As rhythms in music correspond to rhythms in poetry, so musical periods correspond to poetical; and as the most common form of verse is the little four-lined stanza, so the musical period most frequently met with is that consisting of four phrases which correspond, or rhyme, by twos. But musical periods, like poetical stanzas, may consist of six, or eight, or more phrases; or even an irregular number, like five or seven. As in poetry, so in music, a great variety of both rhythms and periods is found.

A period may be divided into sections of (usually) two phrases each; generally two, the first commonly ending with a half-close —that is, a pause on the dominant harmony, while the full close is, of course, on the tonic chord.* The close and the half-close corre-

Half-close. Full-close.

spond to punctuation marks—the full close corresponding to full stop, or period, and the half-close to comma or semicolon. These cadences, the close and the half-close, which are a very important factor in the definition of form, are also one of its earliest indications in popular music.

MOTIVES.

---

* The tonic is the first note of a scale, the key-note; the dominant is the fifth of the same scale or key.

A motive is the shortest possible complete musical idea—it may consist of only two or three notes—and motives may be modified in many ways and yet be recognizable by the rhythm and relative positions of the notes.*

Melodies are constructed from repetitions of motives arranged in phrases, sections and periods.

Before the development of forms founded upon distinct melodic periods, instrumental music was largely constructed from motives arranged in sequences. A sequence is the

---

* It has been estimated that a motive may appear in no less than *eighty-seven* transformations.

repetition of a definite group of notes (or chords) on different degrees of the scale.

When instrumental music began to have an independent existence polyphony reigned, and the ideal type of form was the fugue. It has been already said that polyphonic music is constructed by interweaving melodies, each of which is independent and complete in itself, and all of which are equally important. In homophonic, monodic music, on the contrary, the composition is dominated by a single melody to which everything else is subordinated. Any modern song is a homophonic composition. The accompaniment may be varied in many ways—the harmonies changed, the figures altered—without specially affecting the vocal melody which constitutes the song; but in a polyphonic work the slightest change in any single part influences the whole composition.

A fugue is a polyphonic composition in which a subject—that is, one short theme or phrase—announced by one voice or part is repeated, or answered, by all the others in succession; not strictly, as in a canon, but with various modifications and interruptions. These repetitions, or answers, are called imitations, and these imitations may vary considerably from the original phrase while yet retaining its general form. In a canon the imitations may be at any indicated interval, but in a fugue they are chiefly between the tonic (the first note of the scale) and the dominant (the fifth of the same scale, or key). Indeed, the main distinction between a fugue and other kinds of polyphonic writing is that the former seems to be based upon the relations of tonic and dominant. The name fugue is from the Latin *fugare*—to put to flight—the parts appearing to chase the subject throughout the piece. First one voice part enters alone with the subject in the key of the tonic; then a second voice enters with the answer, which is the subject transposed from tonic to dominant, and sometimes slightly modified to avoid modulating out of the key; and the other voices follow, alternately tonic and dominant, until all have entered. This is called the exposition of the fugue.

After the exposition the composer proceeds to develop all the musical possibilities of the subject in what are termed episodes. He may present the succession of notes which forms the subject, inverted, or backward, augmented — that is, in longer notes than those in the original phrase—or diminished —that is, in shorter notes—and with imitations of every kind, using any of the manifold devices of the art of counterpoint. At intervals throughout the piece the subject is reintroduced and followed by the answer, which sometimes overlaps or interrupts. Such an interruption is called a 'stretto.' Toward the close there is often a pedal or organ point—that is, a long note sustained by one voice while the others proceed in harmonies of which this note does not always form a part. The only notes that can be thus held are the tonic and the dominant, and they are sometimes held together, which is called a double pedal.

The following is the plan of a fugue in D major from Bach's 'Well-tempered Clavichord.' (Czerny—Peters edition—No. 5.—Tausig, No. 3.)

The horizontal lines are not a staff—although the perpendicular lines represent bars—but indicate the four parts or voices, soprano, alto, tenor and bass, with which the fugue is woven. The red mark denotes the subject and the blue the answer, and by

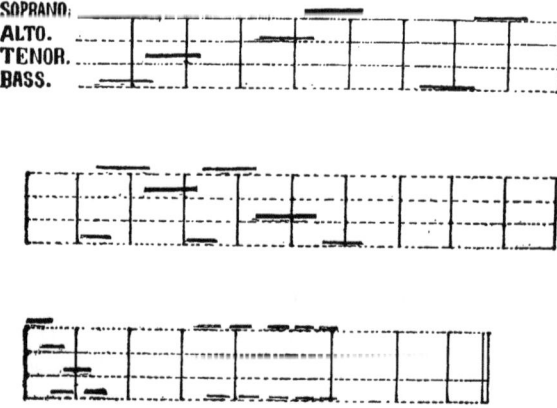

PLAN OF FUGUE.

means of these the construction of the fugue, exposition, episodes and strettos, may easily be followed.

The historian Ambros says that modern music is as much indebted to the dance-tunes which were played by the despised mediæval town-piper as to all the contrapuntal ingenuities of the Netherlanders. It is from the dance-tune that modern musical forms have been developed. The earliest instrumental music of a definite character consisted of arrangements of short dances, and these became in the seventeenth century universally popular. Wandering minstrels carried the national characteristic types from land to land, and they were accepted everywhere—not merely as accompaniments for dancing, but also by the best composers as a basis for artistic instrumental compositions. In these the advantage of contrasting one dance-tune with another was soon perceived, and by the beginning of the eighteenth century the 'allemande,' 'courante,' 'sarabande' and 'gigue' had been grouped into the art-form known as the partita, or suite. This was the first instrumental form in which several movements were combined into a complete whole, and was the direct precursor of the sonata, from which, in early examples, it is often distinguished only in name.

These four dances were usually preceded by a prelude, and between the sarabande and the gigue other dances were frequently introduced, the most familiar of which are the 'gavotte,' 'bourrée,' 'minuet,' 'chaconne' and 'passecaille.' The allemande, which is in common time, is a quiet, moderate movement.

The courante, which follows and contrasts with it, is in three-quarter time, of light and quick movement and full of running passages.* The sarabande is in slow triple time, with a strong emphasis on the second beat of the measure; and the gigue which concludes the series is a lively movement having usually six, nine, or twelve beats to the measure, or, if in quadruple time, so many triplets that the character of the rhythm is maintained.

Of the dances which are occasionally found in the suite, the gavotte is in common time, beginning on the latter half of the measure. The bourrée closely resembles the gavotte, but begins on the last quarter instead of the last half of the measure. The minuet, which is in triple time, is usually followed by a second minuet called in early examples alternativo, because it precedes the repetition of the first, and afterward trio—probably because this second minuet was written in three-part counterpoint.†

---

* This is the Italian courante. The French courante, which sometimes takes its place, is in $\frac{3}{2}$ time and less fluent.

† The part corresponding to this alternativo is still, even in modern dances and marches, called trio, although the name has no longer any significance in respect to the form.

The chaconne and passecaille are both in triple time. The chaconne is a set of variations on a ground bass—that is, a short phrase which is constantly repeated in the bass—and the passecaille differs from it chiefly in that the constantly recurring phrase is not confined to the bass, but appears sometimes in the other parts.

In the suite all the movements are in the same key, and each is based upon a persistent dance rhythm. The sonata differs from the suite in having the various movements in different, though related, keys, in the idealization of the dance rhythms, and also in having the first movement in what is known as first movement, or sonata, form. The first movements of symphonies, concertos, string quartets, trios, etc., are, with few exceptions, written in this form — whence the name, first movement form. When the composition is for either one or two instruments it is called a sonata, but a work in the same form for more than two instruments is usually named according to their number — trio, quartet, quintet, sextet, septet, octet, etc.—and when the composition is for an orchestra it is termed a symphony; a symphony, therefore, being really a sonata for orchestra.

Plan of a First Movement in the Sonata Form.

I. Exposition....... { I. First subject, in the key of the movement.
II. Second subject, in the key of the dominant. }

II. Development.... { III. Working out. }

III. Recapitulation. { IV. First subject, in the key of the movement.
V. Second subject, transposed from the dominant into the key of the movement. }

A sonata first movement consists of three parts: first, the exposition, in which the themes or subjects are presented;* second, the development of these themes by all the musical devices at the command of the composer; † third, the recapitulation of the subjects announced in the first part, the second subject being transposed into the key of the movement. A first movement has five divisions: I. The first subject, in the key of the movement; II. The second subject, in the

---

* This is always followed by the double bar with repeat dots.

† This section is called the working out because the composition is carried on by working over and developing the musical possibilities of the figures and phrases of the principal subjects. It is called also the fantasia, or free part, because here the modulation is entirely unrestricted.

key of the dominant; III. The working out, fantasia, or free part; IV. The return of the first subject in the key of the movement, as at first; V. The return of the second subject in the key of the movement, instead of in the dominant as before. A first movement in a minor key usually has the second subject in the relative major—that is, the major key with the same signature and having its tonic, or key-note, a minor third * higher. At its return the second subject may appear either in the key of the movement, when its intervals must be altered so as to change it from major to minor, or in the major key of the tonic; in which case it is simply transposed, no alteration being needed. In any but the very simplest examples of the sonata form, such as are usually termed sonatinas, this outline, or framework, is very much amplified. There are always in both the first and last sections (exposition and recapitulation) connecting passages between the first and second subjects—that in the first section effecting the modulation from tonic to dominant, or relative major, which in the recapitulation is not required—and the second division, as well as the entire movement, generally ends

---
* Three semitones, or half-steps.

with a coda ; which is a passage added on to emphasize the close. (Compare the sonata in D major by Haydn—Peters edition, No. 7.—Cotta, No. 4.)

Plan of First Movement.

Division I. Measures 1-8. First subject, in D major.
" 9-16. Connecting passage.
Division II. " 17-35. Second subject, in A (the dominant key).
" 35-40. Coda, in A :‖
Division III. " 41-60. Working out.
Division IV. " 61-74. Return of first subject (extended).
" 74-79. Connecting passage.
Division V. " 80-98. Return of second subject, in D.
" 98-103. Coda, in D.

Compare also the sonata by Beethoven in F minor, Op. 2, No. 1.

Plan of First Movement.

Division I. Measures 1-8. First subject, in F minor.
" 8-20. Connecting passage.
Division II. " 20-41. Second subject, in A flat (relative major).
" 41-48. Coda, in A flat. :‖
Division III. " 48-100. Working out.

Division IV. Measures 101–108. Return of first subject.
" 108–119. Connecting passage.
Division V. " 119–140. Return of second subject, in F minor.
" 140–152. Coda, in F minor.

The slow movement of a sonata is usually in what is termed 'song form;' consisting of a first part, second and contrasting part, repetition of the first part and coda. This is called also primary form, in contradistinction to first movement or sonata form, which is called binary. The slow movement of a sonata is, however, sometimes in first movement form, and occasionally it consists of a theme and variations. In early examples it is almost always in the key of the sub-dominant—the fifth below the tonic.

The minuet, which was introduced into the symphony by Haydn, is in the form of the old-fashioned dance—in triple time, with a trio followed by the repetition of the first part. But, though retaining the form, in character the symphonic minuet differs greatly from the dignified movement in which it originated. It becomes constantly lighter and quicker, and is finally transformed into the scherzo by Beethoven, who gave the movement a permanent position in the symphony.

The last movement of a sonata is invariably in the key of the first movement, though one may be in the minor and the other in the major mode, and it is usually in rondo form. A rondo has one principal subject which recurs several times, the intervening passages being termed episodes.*

A first movement differs from a rondo in having *two* principal subjects and a working out.

The name sonata, which means 'sound-piece,' at first merely distinguished the piece that was played from cantata, the piece that was sung. The words 'sonata,' 'canzona' and 'sinfonia' were originally applied to instrumental compositions of all kinds, without designating any particular form. Praetorius says (about 1620): "'Sonata a sonando' is so named because it is to be performed not with men's voices but with instruments alone, after the manner of a canzona. In my opinion the difference between them is this: a sonata is a dignified and stately composition in the style of a mottet, while a canzona is composed with many black notes, is gay and

---

* It is called a rondo because it comes round to the subject after each episode.

joyous and of quick movement throughout."

The violin was the first instrument to attain perfection, the violins of almost three centuries ago being still regarded as unsurpassable models, and with the perfecting of the instrument was developed the great school of Italian violin playing. In Italy in the seventeenth century composers were almost invariably violinists, just as at present they are usually pianists, and sonata was a generally accepted term for violin compositions. Violin sonatas were divided into two classes: the 'sonata da chiesa,' which was really intended for performance in the church service, and the 'sonata da camera,' or secular sonata. This latter was often nothing but a suite of dances, and even the more stately and dignified sonata da chiesa bore no resemblance to the modern sonata beyond the alternation of quick and slow movements.

But when all Italy was so fascinated by the monodic style that her composers, trusting entirely to their natural talents, neglected the study of composition, the true culture of the real art of music was transferred from the south to the north, and it was in Germany that the sonata was developed into the form which is now known by that name. A famous old German organist, Johann Kuhnau (1667-1722), the predecessor of Bach at the Thomas school at Leipsic, is generally regarded as the originator of the clavier sonata; that is, a composition in several movements, not dance-tunes. The great favor with which Kuhnau's sonatas were received encouraged the production of similar works, and in these compositions—in which the number of movements varies from three to eight or more—the old strictly contrapuntal style gradually disappeared, and was replaced by definite melodies accompanied by harmonic figures or chords. Matheson, in his 'Complete Chapelmaster' (published in 1739), says: "During the past few years musicians have composed clavier sonatas with good success; however, they have not as yet the right form, and they aim rather to move the fingers than to touch the heart. In the various movements of a sonata there must be a certain complaisance which suits itself to every hearer. The mourner must find something mournful and sympathetic, the joyful hearer something joyful, the impetuous person something vehement and exciting. Such must be the aim of the composer in writing his adagio, andante, presto, etc., and so will his work succeed." From which it appears that in Matheson's opinion a sonata in addition to a regular form should have also a definite signification and character.

In early sonatas the most common form of first movement is one that is found also in many of the old dances in the suites or partitas. The first half of the piece begins with a definite subject in the tonic, modulates over into the dominant and closes in that key; and the second half begins in the dominant—frequently with the inversion of the subject—and modulates back into the tonic. The modern binary form, having two distinct and contrasting themes or subjects in definitely related tonalities, is dimly foreshadowed here and there in the works of older composers, but was not clearly defined until the time of Haydn (1732–1809) and Mozart (1756–91).

In the development of the sonata the most important predecessor of Haydn was Carl Philipp Emanuel Bach (1713–88), son of the great John Sebastian. He definitely established the sonata as a composition consisting of three movements: the first, an allegro in the sonata form as it was known in his day; the second, an andante or adagio of contrasting character; and the third, a lively rondo. It was by diligent study of the works of Emanuel Bach that Haydn developed the form which has served as a model for all succeeding composers. Haydn said: "For all that I know I am indebted to Carl Philipp Emanuel Bach." And Mozart said: "He is the father, we are the children; whoever among us can do anything has learned it from him."

In the works of Haydn and Mozart the sonata form is fully developed and definitely fixed. With both these composers form predominates, as was indeed not unnatural while the form was yet a novelty. At first it was indispensable that the periods and sections should be clearly and precisely defined; and if the themes were beautiful it was sufficient to connect them by brilliant passages, no matter how meaningless. It remained for Beethoven (1770-1827) to show how the external structure might be dominated by the musical sentiment. Beethoven composed almost exclusively in the sonata form, and expanded its limits in all directions. He exercised much greater freedom in the choice of keys than any of his predecessors—not only for the different movements, but also for the subjects of his first movements. He developed the coda, which with Haydn and Mozart is rarely more than a brilliant flourish, into one of the most beautiful and important parts of the movement, and made the connecting passages an integral part of the whole; so that a work of Beethoven is like an organic growth—each phrase or passage leading naturally and irresistibly to that which follows, and all combining to form a complete and living whole. With Beethoven the sonata form reached its highest development. Though it has been successfully used by later composers, none has done anything to make it a more perfect vehicle for the expression of musical thought.

IX

Precursors of the Piano-forte

THE principal instruments having strings and played by means of a key-board which preceded the piano-forte were the harpsichord, or spinet, and the clavichord; and *all* such instruments, of whatever name, shape, or size, belonged to one or the other of the classes represented by these two, which differed from one another radically in the means by which the sound was produced, in the quality of their tones, and in their derivation from yet older instruments. In the harpsichord the sound was produced by plucking or twanging the strings, as in a harp, by points of some hard substance elevated on wooden uprights called jacks and raised by the depression of the keys. In the clavichord, on the contrary, the sound was produced by the pressure against the string of small brass wedges called tangents, which served not only to excite its vibrations but at the same time shortened the vibrating length and fixed the pitch of the tone; so that the clavichord, like the violin, was tuned in

MONOCHORD.
From the Micrologus of Guido d'Arezzo. Manuscript copy of the twelfth century.

the act of playing, while in the harpsichord the tone was fixed, as in the piano-forte.

The clavichord, which is the older of the two instruments, had its origin in the monochord; which was at first, as its name implies, a single string stretched over a sound-board and measured off into vibrating lengths by a movable bridge.

MONOCHORD.
From the Theorica Musice (1490) of Franchinus Gafurius.

On the sound-board under the string were marked the divisions corresponding to the different degrees of the scale; if the whole length of the string gave the tone G, eight-ninths would give the tone A; four-fifths

would give B; three-quarters C; two-thirds
D; etc. With this one-stringed instrument,
of course, no two tones could ever be sounded
together. Very early, therefore, other strings
were added, all tuned in unison and each
furnished with its own movable bridge. In
the earliest monochords the strings were
stretched by means of weights, and Greek
theoreticians mention such instruments with
as many as four strings. A primitive sort of
key-board, which had been already applied to
the organ, was early applied also to the monochord. To the inner end of the key-lever
was attached an upright wedge, like a flat-
tened pin, which, when the key was de-
pressed by the finger, struck the string, set
it in vibration and at the same time shortened
it to the length indicated by the position of
the key; thus taking the place of the movable
bridge. Guido d' Arezzo, who lived in the
eleventh century and was a famous music-
teacher, advises students to "exercise the
hand in the use of the monochord," and from
this it has been inferred that there were in
his day monochords with some sort of a key-
board. But the only definite information we
have concerning early musical instruments is
from representations in sculpture and painting

and descriptions in books, and the earliest mention of a clavichord is in the year 1404. It is impossible to fix exactly the date of its invention, which, however, the historian Ambros thinks cannot be earlier than the middle of the fourteenth century.

There is a rare and curious old book entitled 'Musica getutscht und ausgezogen durch Sebastianum Virdung, Priesters von Amberg,'* which is the oldest work describing the precursors of modern musical instruments. It was published in 1511, is illustrated with wood-cuts, and begins with a description of key-board instruments showing distinctly the difference between the two classes represented by clavichord and harpsichord. Virdung describes the oldest monochord known to him as having twenty white keys, from G to $\bar{\bar{e}}$, and in each of the upper two octaves a single black key for the tone B flat—which was necessary for the Guidonian system of hexachords. Seven strings were sufficient to allow these twenty-two tones to be heard, and these strings were all tuned in unison to the lowest tone of the instrument, G, which was sounded by the first key causing the whole

---

* Music Depicted and Set Forth by Sebastian Virdung, Priest of Amberg.

length of the string to vibrate. The second key shortened the same string by a ninth and sounded A; the third shortened it by a fifth and sounded B; but the tangent of the fourth key touched the second string, and shortening it by one-quarter gave the tone C; etc. A strip of cloth, which was the common damper for all the strings, prevented the vibration of that portion which was not desired to sound.

Since the tones G, A and B were all produced from the same string, they of course could never be sounded together, and in the lowest octave the first possible accord would be G C. But with the growing appreciation of harmony it became necessary to have at least so many strings that all the consonances of the ecclesiastical modes, which were then exclusively in use, might be sounded. However, even when clavichords were manufactured with key-boards on which the white and black keys alternated as they do at present, the tangents of three or four different keys produced their tones from one and the same string by causing different lengths of it to vibrate. These clavichords were called 'gebunden,' and it was not until the eighteenth century that a so-called 'bundfrei' clavichord was manufactured, having a separate string for each key.

The clavichord always retained its original shape—derived from the monochord—that of a long, rectangular box, which at first stood upon a table but was finally provided with feet of its own, and, despite the fact that the number of both keys and strings was con-

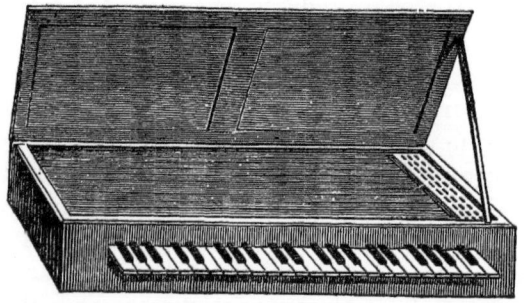

stantly increased, this instrument continued to be known as a monochord down into the sixteenth century, when it begins to be called clavichord.*

The early clavichords had all the strings of the same length, and this had one great advantage: when the bridges or tangents were once fixed exactly in the required places it was only necessary to keep the strings tuned

---

* From clavis, a key, and chorda, string.

in unison. But as the compass of the instruments increased this was found to be inconvenient, and finally a long, wooden bridge was placed diagonally under the strings, which were turned around small pegs and so gradually shortened up to the highest tone. The introduction of the bridge made

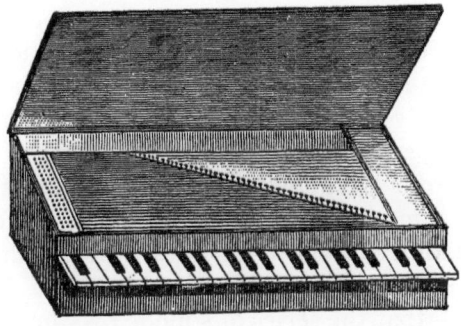

it possible to give to the upper tones not only shorter but at the same time thinner strings, and to the lower tones longer and heavier ones. The thinner the string the greater must be its length in order to produce a given tone. If the bass strings of modern pianos were no thicker than those in the treble they would have to be enormously long in proportion. Consequently, as the compass of the key-board increased it became more and more desirable to be able to use strings of greater weight for the bass and lesser for the treble; and this, of course, involved the giving up of the unisonal tuning.

With the giving up of the unison of the strings and the gradual superseding of the ecclesiastical modes by the modern tonalities, began that series of experiments in search of a rule for the tuning of instruments of fixed intonation, which occupied both theoreticians and practical musicians for many decades, and finally resulted in the universal adoption of the system of equal temperament.

In order to understand what is meant by equal temperament it is indispensable to disabuse our minds of the idea—the result of early familiarity with the piano-forte keyboard—that the series of sounds produced by striking in succession the row of white keys from C to C is the natural, or true, scale. That series of sounds comprises two consecutive whole tones, or steps, a semitone, or half-step, three consecutive whole tones and another semitone.

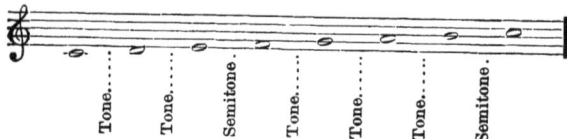

But the intervals of the true major diatonic scale really are the following:

a greater tone, a lesser tone, a semitone, another greater tone, a lesser tone, a greater tone and another semitone. There are, moreover, in addition to the seven sounds of the diatonic scale, certain chromatic tones, which are only imperfectly represented on the pianoforte key-board. Between C and D are C sharp and D flat—the interval from C to C sharp being greater than that from C to D flat—between G and A are G sharp and A flat, and so on. The twelve scales or keys which are in common use require eleven chromatic, in addition to the seven diatonic, tones, making eighteen within the compass of a single octave. The human voice can, of course, produce all these tones, no matter how small the intervals which separate them, and instruments like the violin and trombone also can be played with just intonation: because the player can modify the pitch as he pleases. But with instruments whose tones are fixed, like the piano and organ, the pitch does not depend upon the player, but upon the tuner, and the number of tones in the octave being limited, if some scales are tuned perfectly certain tones which belong to other scales will be missing. If, on such an instrument, the scale of C is tuned correctly according to the standard of the true major diatonic scale, given above, every other scale will be out of tune; because the intervals will not fit into their proper places in the series. The interval D E, which in the scale of C is the second step and, when the scale is perfectly tuned, smaller than the first step, must in the scale of D serve for the first step, which should be the larger; and so with all the other intervals.

Numerous experiments have been made which endeavored to supply on key-board instruments the number of tones in the octave necessary to produce all the scales with just intonation. Zarlino (1517–93), the most ingenious and progressive theoretician of his day, describes an instrument which he had made. Its compass was but two octaves, and the lower, or white, keys were arranged as they are at the present time. Between B and C, however, and E and F, were keys in form and position like our black ones, but white in color, and between all the ther lower keys were pairs of upper ones of which one was black and the other white; so that in each octave instead of twelve there were nineteen keys, representing as many different tones. " But," says Zarlino, " even by the addition of many more it would never be possible to attain perfect purity of all intervals, nor to produce more agreeable consonances than those already known." About the same time another instrument was manufactured having five key-boards one above another, and upon this, it is said, all scales could be perfectly tuned.

The impracticability of manufacturing and of tuning such instruments, to say nothing of the immense difficulty of playing upon them, effectually prevented their general use, and efforts were made to attain by other means the desired end; that of producing upon the same instrument all the scales with an equal degree of purity—or impurity, as many of the musicians of the time considered it. From the sixteenth century onward experiments in tuning were constantly made in the endeavor to attain this end with only twelve keys to the octave. Innumerable methods were proposed—and opposed—and many books published, in which, as Matheson, writing in the eighteenth century, says: "As much ado is made about it as if the welfare of the whole world depended upon the tuning of a single clavier."

Rameau was the first to propose a really practical system—that which, in principle at least, is followed by the tuners of the present day. By this, the difference between C and the B sharp at which we arrive in following a succession of twelve consecutive fifths upward is evenly divided between all the intervening fifths, so that the B sharp stands to C in the relation of an octave; and the same with the difference between C and the D flat which we find by following a succession of twelve fifths downward. As this difference is only about one-fifth of a semitone, each fifth loses only about one-sixtieth; a comparatively small deviation from the absolute purity of the interval. Tuning by equal temperament is really a system of compromise—what is taken from one interval being added to another—the result being the division of the octave into twelve equal parts, each of which differs but slightly from the corresponding interval of the true scale. One of these parts

Precursors of the Piano-forte 161

is taken as the standard of measurement for a semitone, and two for a whole tone, and on an instrument of fixed intonation tuned by this

PSALTERY.
From the painting by Orcagna, in the National Gallery, London.

duodecimal division of the octave a scale consisting of steps and half-steps will fit anywhere.

The method of tuning by equal temperament is now almost universally applied to instruments with fixed tones—though even in modern times organs have been built with key-boards on which the black keys are divided, one-half producing the flat, and the other the sharp, tone. " There can be no question," says Helmholtz, " that the system of tuning by equal temperament has, by its extreme simplicity, extraordinary advantages for instrumental music; that any other system would necessitate a very complicated mechanism and increase in proportion the difficulties of performance; and that, therefore, the high development of instrumental music has become possible only by the general adoption of the system of tempered tuning." Without this system modern musical forms, a fundamental principle of which is key relationship and contrast, would be much restricted, and the enharmonic modulations *

---

* The word enharmonic, applied in the Greek system to intervals smaller than a semitone, is in modern music referred to the difference between two tones which on keyed instruments tuned by equal temperament are represented by one and the same sound; as, for instance, C sharp and D flat. If we consider the tone represented in one chord by a sharp as that represented in another chord by a flat we shall have an enharmonic modulation.

that play such an important part in modern compositions would be impossible. The musician who contributed most toward the general adoption of equal temperament was John Sebastian Bach (1685–1750). Bach, who always tuned his own instruments, tested the system in his famous work, 'The Well-tempered Clavichord;' which is a collection, in two parts, of forty-eight preludes and fugues in all keys, major and minor — in each part a prelude and fugue in each key.

The tone of the clavichord, though agreeable and sensitive to the touch of the player, was always feeble and wavering; and the natural desire for an instrument whose strings could be excited to stronger vibrations seems to have resulted in the addition of a keyboard to the psaltery and the production of the class of instruments represented by the harpsichord. The psaltery is a trapeze-shaped instrument played by plucking the strings with the fingers, or with plectra of ivory or

JACK.

metal held in the hand or fastened into rings worn on the fingers of the player. In the harpsichord the strings were set in vibration by points of some hard substance which twitched or plucked them as the depression of the keys forced the points upward; and the jack which twangs the string of the harpsichord corresponds to the plectrum of the psaltery, just as the tangent of the clavichord

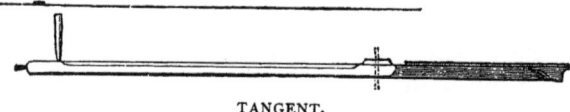

TANGENT.

corresponds to the bridge of the monochord. About the end of the fifteenth century quills were substituted for the points of shell or ivory which had previously been used, and from that time the instrument was known also by the name of spinet.*

The virginal, which was identical with the spinet, received its name, according to an ancient lexicographer, " because maids and virgins do most commonly play on them." The

---

* From spina, a thorn or point, though the name has also been derived from Spinetti, who was a manufacturer of musical instruments.

long harpsichords, like a grand piano, were sometimes described as spinet or virginal, but the rectangular instruments were never called harpsichords. In France the harpsichord was called claveçin. Early stringed instruments with key-boards were made in many shapes and sizes and known by many names— clavicymbel, clavicytherium, clavicembalo (or simply cembalo), arpicordo, etc. (see illustrations at the end of this volume), but whatever the

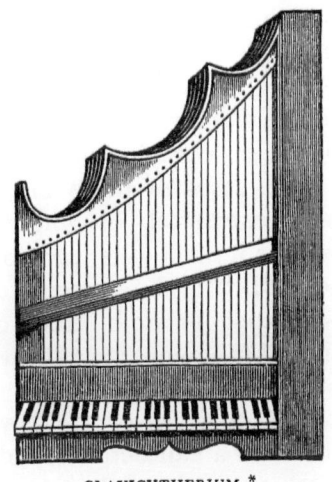

CLAVICYTHERIUM.*

From 'Musica getutscht und ausgezogen' (1511) by Sebastian Virdung.

---

* The shorter strings are, apparently, opposite the bass keys, and the longer opposite the treble. For this seeming irregularity of construction the responsibility rests with the sixteenth century artist, who has drawn the instrument upon the wood exactly as it appeared to him—the impression, of course, showing everything reversed.

variations in shape or nomenclature they can all be referred to the two classes of clavichord and harpsichord; that is, instruments on which the sound was produced by pressure and shortening of the string by means of tangents, and instruments on which the sound was produced by plucking the strings by means of jacks and quills.

The cases of these old instruments were often exquisitely ornamented; carved, inlaid with ivory and other precious substances, and sound-board, cover and side-panels decorated with appropriate mottoes, or paintings by artists of renown. (See illustrations at the end of this volume.)

The compass of the key-board was about four and a half octaves, and in the older German instruments the natural keys are often black and the sharps white; the Italian rule being the reverse:

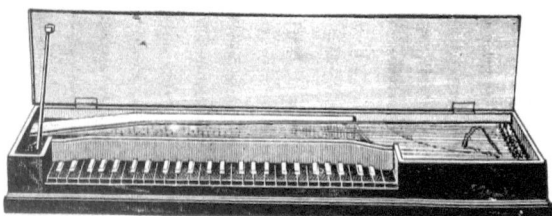

With instruments whose strings were made to vibrate by being twitched, or plucked, modification of tone by means of touch was not possible; but some of these instruments possessed considerable power. The harpsichord was the most important of all the keyed instruments that preceded the piano-forte, and until nearly the close of the last century it had a place in the orchestra. Harpsichord playing was most esteemed in France and Italy, while in Germany the clavichord was always the favorite instrument. The clavichord was comparatively inexpensive, easily tuned and kept in order, while the cost of tuning a harpsichord and renewing the quills must have been considerable. This may have contributed to recommend the former to the frugal German mind, but in any case the fact remains that the "gentle and intimate clavichord" was always the favorite instrument in German households. An old German lexicographer characterizes the clavichord as "the comfort of the sufferer and the sympathizing friend of cheerfulness." Its tone, though weak and tremulous, could be varied by the touch of the player, while the tone of the harpsichord was monotonous and always staccato. From the clavichord both staccato and legato effects might be obtained, and by an intermittent pressure of the finger a continuous repetition of the tone could be produced.

This effect, which was called 'bebung,' was much admired. Carl Philipp Emanuel Bach (1713-88) in his work on 'The true Art of Playing the Clavier' says: "I believe that a good clavichord possesses, with the exception of its weaker tone, all the beauties of the piano-forte, and in addition the 'bebung.'" He says also that the clavichord is the instrument upon which one can best form his judgment of a player. The clavichord undoubtedly required more nicety of execution than the harpsichord, and the greater capacity of the instrument for expressive playing demanded correspondingly greater capacity in the performer. Matheson, writing in the early part of the eighteenth century, says that "for the clavichord one must have a delicate hand and execute all the ornaments distinctly, while upon the harpsichord, with its loud and echoing tones, much slovenly playing will be passed over." The clavichord was the favorite instrument of the great Bach, and even Beethoven is reported to have said that on the clavichord one could best control tone and expression.

Precursors of the Piano-forte 169

The pedal, which was first used to double the bass tones of the organ, was early applied to the clavier and connected with dampers for producing different degrees and qualities of tone. There were also contrivances worked by the knees of the player, like the swell in the modern reed organ, and stops for different registers, couplers and other organ devices. The shifting key-board also was an early invention. Praetorius describes an instrument of the sixteenth century on which the key-board could be moved four semitones to the right, so that a composition might be easily transposed from C into E or any of the intervening keys. In the course of the eighteenth century inventions and combinations of all kinds were applied to keyed instruments with strings; some to vary the quality of tone or increase its duration, some to produce crescendo or diminuendo effects; but most of them seem to have endeavored by means of stops to imitate all the tones of the full orchestra. Various keyed instruments also were invented which sought to produce sustained tone by some application of the principle of the bow. In some of these the strings were made to vibrate by being rubbed with small wheels; in others, the depression of the key pressed the string against a bow of horse-hair, the motion of which was controlled by a pedal; but as the piano-forte gradually approached perfection it drove all its rivals from the field.

The piano-forte * was invented in Florence about the year 1710 by a harpsichord maker named Bartolomei Christofori. As the harpsichord seems to have been derived from the

psaltery, and the clavichord from the monochord, so the piano-forte shows clearly its connection with the dulcimer; which is an instrument almost identical in construction with the psaltery, but played in an entirely different manner—the strings of the dulcimer being struck with small hammers, while in the psaltery the sound is produced by plucking the strings.†

---

* Piano e forte—soft and loud.
† The dulcimer is the cymbal of the Hungarian gypsies.

Indeed, the performances of a celebrated virtuoso upon the dulcimer, Pantaleon Hebenstreit, seem to have suggested in more than one mind the possibility of substituting hammers for the jack of the harpsichord. Although the honor of being the inventor of the piano-forte belongs to Christofori, to Gottfried Silbermann, of Dresden, is due the credit of the development and improvement which first rendered its acceptance by musicians in any degree general. The mechanism of the early models was very imperfect, and good harpsichords were preferable to poor piano-fortes. Silbermann, who seems to have had great perseverance and tenacity of purpose, spent the larger portion of his working years in effort and experiment toward the improvement of the piano-forte. Agricola, Bach's pupil, says: "With him all workmanship must be genuine and good; he would have nothing for show, and defective work, even finished piano-fortes, he destroyed." The same writer goes on to say: "Herr Silbermann at first finished two of these instruments, one of which the late Herr Capellmeister, Herr Johann Sebastian Bach, examined and played upon. He admired and praised the tone, but censured the weakness of the upper notes and the heaviness of the action. This criticism Herr Silbermann, who could never endure to have any fault found with his work, took very ill, and kept for a long time his anger against Herr Bach. Nevertheless, his conscience told him that Herr Bach was right, and he held it for better not to give out any more of these instruments, but strove industriously to correct the faults which Herr Bach had pointed out. To this end he labored many years, and that this was the true reason of his delay he candidly acknowledged to me himself. Finally, however, Herr Silbermann, having really made many improvements, sold one of these instruments to the court at Rudolstadt, and shortly after his Majesty the King of Prussia ordered several " (which are yet in the various palaces at Potsdam). " On all these instruments could be seen and heard, particularly by those who, like myself, had already seen the older ones, how industriously and perseveringly Herr Silbermann had labored for their improvement. Herr Silbermann had also the praiseworthy ambition to show one of these later instruments to the Herr Capellmeister Bach, and obtained from him the fullest approbation."

Although the greatest musicians acknowledged the value of the piano-forte, it was many years before it took the rank which it deserved; the main reason being, probably, that the new instrument demanded a new technique. The first writer who notices Christofori's invention says: "Many musicians will not give to this instrument the praise which is due, because the tone is too soft and dull; although one becomes easily accustomed to it, and soon prefers the piano-forte to all other instruments. But the chief objection which is raised is this: that one must learn to play upon it after an entirely new fashion, even if one is already well practised in playing upon other keyed instruments. Being, however, an entirely new invention, it is, of course, necessary first to study its nature in order to bring forth with taste and skill its special excellencies." Prejudice never yields so slowly as when supported by habit. A writer in the year 1782 says: "With the harpsichord the heart cannot speak—there is no light nor shade, but only a clear, definite outline. The piano-forte stands higher, especially if it be a good instrument. With it the heart can already speak, and express with its light and shade manifold emotions. But highest of all stands the clavichord. Excluded by its nature from the public concert, it is so much the more the confidant of loneliness and solitude. With the clavichord can the heart give itself fullest expression. To know a virtuoso," he concludes, "one must hear him at the clavichord, not at the piano-forte, least of all at the harpsichord." Another writer says: " The harpsichord exercises the hand after the correct manner, therefore a beginner should first practise on the harpsichord. The piano-forte must be handled very differently, and this instrument is very far from giving all shades of expression. But the clavichord—that solitary, melancholy, unspeakably sweet instrument—has advantages above both. By the pressure of the finger, the trembling of the strings, by the stronger or more delicate touch of the hand, the swelling and diminishing of the tone, the melting trill, the portamento, every impulse of emotion can find expression."

The great step in the construction of the piano-forte was made when metal began to be used, first for strengthening and afterward as the sole material for the frame. This made possible the use of heavy strings under great tension, and such strings give the purest and most brilliant tone. In a modern concert grand the strings exert a force of about 75,000 pounds, and only the solid iron frame preserves the instrument from destruction. The thickest bass string of the first pianos was thinner than the smallest treble string of a modern instrument, and when the only resisting material was wood the tension had to be correspondingly slight. It was not until metal bracing had been successfully applied to the piano-forte that the newer instrument definitely superseded the older ones.

X

Development of Piano-forte Playing

THE technique of the clavier seems to have been at first identical with that of the organ. The early composers apparently recognized no difference, as far as technical treatment was concerned, between the two instruments, and even as late as the seventeenth century music was published with the indication ' for organ *or* clavier ' upon the title-page. It was in Venice, that great commercial republic of the Middle Ages which early became a centre of art and learning, that the difference between organ and clavier seems first to have been definitely recognized. Venice was in the sixteenth century celebrated for her excellent organists, many of whom were known also as clavier players, and one of these, Claudio Merulo, contributed very materially to the formation of a style of composition suited especially to the clavier as distinguished from the organ—his toccatas exhibiting the broken chords, quick runs and lively figures which were peculiarly appropriate to the delicate and evanescent tone of the older instruments.*

Here is a letter written nearly four centuries ago, which proves that even at that early date the clavichord—monochord it was then called—was a favorite instrument in private circles, and that it was even then customary for the daughters of wealthy and cultivated families to learn to play upon it as a part of their regular education. In the sixteenth century such young maidens were generally sent to the convents to be educated, and we know that some of the best organists in Venice were at the same time music-teachers in various convents. About the year 1529 the daughter of Pietro Bembo, well known as a poet and man of letters, wrote to beg permission to share such instruction—to take music-lessons, as we should say—and this is a portion of the father's answer: "Touching thy desire to learn to play upon the monochord,

---

* A toccata—literally a touch piece, as a sonata was a sound piece and a cantata a piece to be sung—was a composition designed to exhibit the technique of the performer.

I answer, since because of thy tender years thou canst not know of thyself, that playing is suited only for vain and frivolous women; but I desire thee to be the purest and most lovable maiden in the world. Moreover, thou wouldst have but little pleasure or renown if thou playedst badly, and to play well it would be necessary for thee to spend ten or twelve years in practice, without being able to think on anything else. Consider for thyself if that would be proper for thee. If now thy friends and companions desire thee to learn to play in order to give them pleasure, so say to them that thou wishest not to make thyself ridiculous before them, and content thyself with learning and handiwork." Bembo's opinions have been shared by many sensible fathers in later times.

Besides the toccatas there were for early clavier players canzone 'per sonar'—to distinguish them from the canzone which were to be sung—and so-called sonatas. There were also the more strictly contrapuntal compositions, canons and fugues, and finally the popular melodies and dance-tunes. These had long been used by composers as the foundation for vocal works, but being spaced off in very long notes and surrounded by the elaborate counterpoint of the other parts, had in such compositions entirely lost all character. But these melodies and dance-tunes arranged simply for clavier became extremely popular, and from them was developed the artistic partita or suite.

Until the seventeenth century all music was constructed contrapuntally—that is, all the parts or voices were independent, and each complete in itself. There were as many staves as voices, and these were not always written one over the other, but sometimes even on different pages of the book; so that the difficulty for the player who had to unite these separate voices in chords was great.* To facilitate this task a series of bass notes

* The concentration of all the parts upon a system of two staves only, as in modern piano-forte music, dates from the latter part of the seventeenth century

called basso continuo, or thoroughbass, was provided, and to this were added the figures and signs of transposition indicating the chords, from which it afterward received the name of figured bass. For nearly two centuries oratorios and operas were always accompanied by organ or harpsichord, in addition to the other instruments, and the accompanist was expected to construct the harmonies from this basso continuo, or figured bass, which was all that was ever furnished by the composer; so the study of this branch of musical art became a very important part in the education of every organ and clavier player.

Toward the close of the sixteenth century the first regular instruction-book for clavier and organ was published at Venice. In this the author, Girolamo Diruta, draws especial attention to the difference between clavier and organ playing, and gives rules for the position of the hands and for fingering. At that time, and for long afterward, the thumb and little finger were almost never used in playing. In fingering the scales the right hand, ascending, used alternately the middle and ring fingers—descending, the middle and forefingers; for the left hand the rule was the reverse. This kind of fingering was not altogether unreasonable as applied to the in-

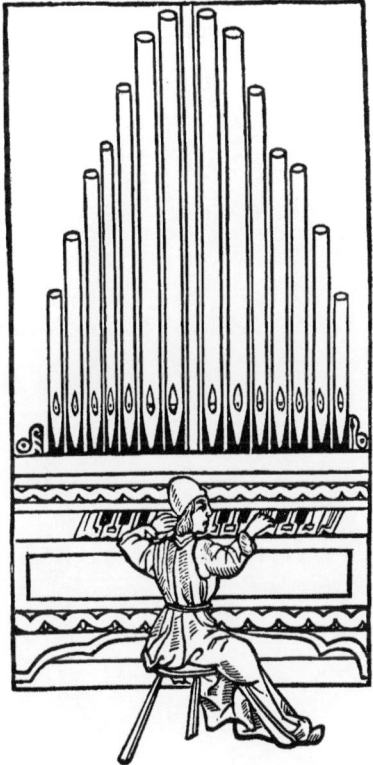

struments then in use. The key-boards of the earlier organs were so high above the seat of the player that the elbows were considerably lower than the hands, and music for both organ and clavier, which were then not tuned by equal temperament, was written

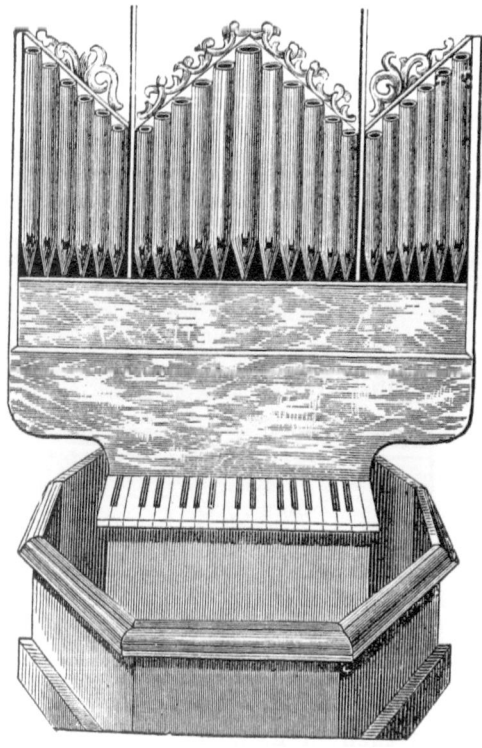

ORGAN WITH PROJECTING KEYBOARD.
From an early sixteenth century picture.

in only the simplest tonalities; so that the black keys were but seldom required. Moreover, the tone was produced by pressure, and this could best be applied by the three longer fingers straightened out; while the thumb and little finger would be below the level of the key-board, which in the older instruments projected beyond the framework.

But in the early part of the eighteenth century three great players in three different countries — France, Italy, and Germany — revolutionized existing methods. These were François Couperin (1668–1733), Domenico Scarlatti (1683–1757) and John Sebastian Bach (1685–1750), and to them we are chiefly indebted for the definite establishment of a distinct clavier style, and the development in technique of lightness, elegance and grace. Scarlatti, who was a remarkably brilliant and clever player, was the first to introduce a rapid crossing of the hands, running passages in thirds and sixths, quick repetition of a tone by striking the key with successive fingers, and many other technical devices now familiar, but in his day absolutely novel. Couperin, though a less brilliant player than Scarlatti, was a very elegant and refined musician. His melodies are profusely ornamented with all those graceful turns, trills, etc., by which the early composers endeavored to disguise the thin tone of the older instruments, and he was one of the first to give to instrumental compositions distinctive titles expressive of the character of the music. Couperin was also one of the first to use the thumb in playing, and in his work, 'L'Art de toucher du Claveçin,' gives numerous, though irregular, examples of its employment. But to John Sebastian Bach, who was by far the greatest genius of the three, fingering owes its development into a system. He fixed the place of the thumb in the scale, and made free use of both that and the little finger, raising the wrists and curving the fingers, which in playing, it is said, he drew gently inward without moving the rest of the hand. We must remember, however, that the instrument upon which Bach habitually played was the clavichord, the tone of which was produced by pressure, not by the blow necessitated by the hammer of the piano-forte, which compels the raising of the fingers. The clavichord was Bach's favorite instrument. He said that he found no soul in the claveçin, or spinet, and the early piano-fortes, the mechanism of which was still imperfect, he thought clumsy and harsh.

Before the piano-forte came into general use clavier technique was already highly developed and the literature of key-board instruments both extensive and valuable. But the quality of the tone produced and the limitations of the technique required to produce it unite to determine the character of the music composed for any instrument, and with the perfecting of the piano-forte not only the manner of playing but also the style of composition altered very materially. In the clavichord, the tone of which was produced by pressure of the tangent on the string, the tone might be prolonged by continued pressure, but was always weak and tremulous. Since the key must be kept pressed down as long as the sound was desired to continue, and as too strong a pressure sharpened the pitch of the tone, a brilliant style was hardly to be cultivated on the clavichord. But on the more brilliant harpsichord the player had absolutely no control over the tone beyond the mere staccato twanging of the string by the jack, and fluency and rapidity were the qualities demanded by compositions for that instrument;

while in music for both clavichord and harpsichord a profusion of embellishments was considered necessary to disguise the tonal deficiencies and compensate for the lack of sustained melody. But with the introduction of the hammer, producing a more prolonged tone the dynamic force of which could be controlled by the touch of the player, was gained greater power of expressing personal sentiment; and in compositions for the pianoforte the lyrical element begins to appear.

Carl Philipp Emanuel Bach (1713-88) was the first to practically recognize the change of treatment demanded by the new instrument. In his essay on 'The True Art of Playing the Clavier' he lays much stress upon the importance of a singing style. "Methinks," he says, "music ought principally to move the heart; and in this no performer on the piano-forte will succeed by merely thumping and drumming, or by continual arpeggio playing. During the last few years my chief endeavor has been to play the piano-forte, in spite of its deficiency in sustaining the sound, as much as possible in a singing manner, and to compose for it accordingly."

In this essay, which was the first really important work on clavier playing, he bases fingering on scientific principles. He says that the hands should swing freely in a horizontal position over the key-board, with the fingers curved; that playing with straightened fingers separates the longer ones too far from the thumb, and renders this, which is really the principal finger, incapable of performing its duty. The black keys, which are shorter and lie higher than the white ones, belong naturally to the three longer fingers; and this, he says, is the reason for the first and principal rule—that the little finger is seldom, and the thumb only in case of *absolute necessity*, to be used upon the black keys. He also gives rules for the performance of the numerous ornaments that were so conspicuous in the music of his day, counsels the player to train and develop the left hand equally with the right, advises practice upon the harpsichord, which required more strength of finger than the light-actioned clavichord, and finally treats, with great good sense, of expression and the manner of performance. " Good execution," he remarks, " is the art of so presenting musical thoughts that the hearers shall comprehend their true meaning and emotional content; for by the manner of performance one and the same thought may receive quite different interpretations. Therefore, take not an adagio too quickly nor an allegro too slowly; give to all notes the values which belong to them, and let the execution be everywhere clear, flowing and distinct. From the soul must one play, and not like a trained bird; for a musician cannot touch the feelings of others without being moved by the same feelings himself—he must share all those emotions which he desires to excite in the breasts of his hearers." Emanuel Bach was the representative musician of his day, and as regards both playing and composition he exercised a decided influence. Haydn (1732–1809) and Mozart (1756–91) acknowledged their indebtedness to him, and in all their compositions the lyrical element, upon which he laid such stress, predominates.*

Mozart's contemporaries all testify to the excellence of his playing. Clementi declared that he had never heard anyone play with so much charm as Mozart, and Haydn said that Mozart's playing "went to the heart." "'Three things are necessary for a good performer,' said Mozart, pointing significantly

---

* Mozart was one of the first to compose pieces for two performers at one key-board. Before his day the compass of the instruments was hardly sufficient for this.

to his head, to his heart and to the tips of his fingers, as symbolical of understanding, sympathy and technical skill."

Yet Mozart, with all his genius and charm, was hardly a piano-forte player in the modern sense, his technique being rather that of the harpsichord. The founder of modern piano-forte technique was Muzio Clementi (1752-1832), who may be regarded as the first great piano-forte virtuoso, his compositions heading the list of those that pay the greatest attention to merely mechanical skill. Clementi, who seems to have divined almost by instinct the kind of treatment to which the piano-forte best responds, introduced many technical novelties—passages in double thirds and sixths, runs in octaves, etc. (see his celebrated collection of studies, the 'Gradus ad Parnassum')—and his compositions demand for their performance much greater muscular force and endurance than had been required by anything before his day. Clementi was for many years a partner in an English piano manufacturing firm, and made many important improvements in the construction of the instrument. As his intimate practical acquaintance with every detail of its mechanism enabled him to make use of every technical device for developing to the utmost its resources of tone and brilliancy, so, reciprocally, his immense and ever increasing technique, making constantly greater and greater demands upon the capacity of the instrument, led him continually to improve its mechanism. The compass of the key-board, which had been but five or five and a half octaves, was extended to six and six and a half, and the piano-forte became for the first time powerful and sonorous, well adapted to the playing of sustained melody and vigorous passages.

Beethoven (1770–1827), whose achievements as a composer have quite overshadowed his fame as a pianist, introduced the dramatic element into instrumental music. With Clementi as his model for technical development he acquired the perfect command of the instrument which is necessary for the successful performance of his greatest compositions, but cared nothing for mere brilliancy and polish of execution. One of his pupils says that in the lesson he was " comparatively careless as to the right notes being played, but angry at once at any failure in expression, or in comprehension of the character of the piece; saying that the first might be an accident, but that the other showed want of knowledge, or feeling, or attention." With his extempore playing he roused his audiences to the highest pitch of excitement. Czerny says: " Frequently not an eye remained dry, while many would break out into loud sobs; for there was something wonderful in his expression." Beethoven's playing has been characterized as tone painting and compared to dramatic recitation. Schindler, his friend and biographer, says that in the performance of his piano-forte works Beethoven laid the greatest stress upon the musical declamation; "for," said he, "although the poet in his monologue or dialogue follows a regular and definite rhythm, yet the actor or reciter, to insure a perfect comprehension of the meaning of the poem, makes rests and pauses even where the poet would not venture to indicate them, so must a player employ this art of declamation in his performance of the music." Almost any mature work of Beethoven reveals this dramatic element. In some there are passages of distinct recitative, the words of which we seem almost to hear; in others, the intensity of the passion gives to the music the force of a personal utterance, at times the immensity of the thought even obscuring its expression.

Clementi's most celebrated pupil was the talented Irishman, John Field (1782-1837), whose influence, both as player and composer, has been felt by all later pianists. Clementi kept him in the warerooms to show off the instruments, which at that time were constantly improving in the direction of power and quality of tone, and Field made good use of his opportunities; his touch surpassing, in beauty and sustaining power, all that had been heard before. Liszt says that Field, who was the inventor of the nocturne, was the first to free piano-forte compositions from the fetters of the custom which made it obligatory for such a piece to be a sonata, rondo, or the like. He says: "Field introduced a new race of compositions in which feeling and song predominated, free from the shackles of any superimposed pattern. He opened the way for that long series of 'Songs without Words,' 'Impromptus,' 'Ballades,' etc., which have since appeared, and to him may be traced the origin of all those compositions which seek through the medium of tones to give expression to the most intimate moods and innermost feelings of the soul."

In the first half of the present century

piano-forte technique sustained an extraordinary development. Before its commencement the difference between the piano-forte and its predecessors had been definitely recognized and the principles of fingering established. The construction of the instrument steadily improved, and as its resources became better understood the capacity of the human hand, also, was carefully studied and systematically developed. The heavier action of the newer instruments compelled the lifting of the fingers and demanded increased muscular force, and the quiet position of the older players was gradually superseded by free movements of wrist and arm.

Technical efficiency is the legitimate and necessary means by which a musical work is presented to the hearer; but often what should be only the means is regarded as the end of artistic effort. In the earlier part of this century technical execution was brought to a very high degree of perfection by a number of players who regarded the art of composition merely as affording opportunities for the exhibition of mechanical skill. Thalberg (1812–71) was probably the greatest virtuoso of this class. The perfection of his technique justly commanded admiration, being the result of a diligent and complete training of the fingers upon legitimate principles, but his compositions were almost exclusively bravura pieces intended for the display of his own wonderful manual dexterity.

It was the leaders of the romantic school—Mendelssohn (1809–47), Schumann (1810–56), Chopin (1810–49), Liszt (1811–86)—who finally restored the musical idea to its rightful position of first importance; recognizing virtuosity only as serving to give the clearest and most intelligent expression to the thoughts of the composer. Mendelssohn's influence was felt chiefly through his performance of works of masters greater than himself, and Schumann's in the amount of poetical material with which he enriched the literature of the instrument, but Chopin and Liszt revolutionized piano-forte playing. Chopin's compositions abound in innovations. Players, even the most skilful, trained only in the older methods found their technique quite inadequate to the rendering of Chopin's music. His extended and irregular arpeggios, which sometimes compel the passing of the thumb under the little finger, or the little finger over the thumb, irregular grouping of three, four, five, seven or more notes against two or three, and much of the delicate and fantastic ornamentation of his melodies are entirely original. But his greatest innovations were in the use of the pedal, upon which his most poetic effects depend. The older pianists used the pedal very sparingly; most of their music can be played just as well without it, but its aid is indispensable to the rendering of Chopin's sustained melodies. Chopin, moreover, utilized its capacity for beautifying tone by allowing the sympathetic vibrations of related strings.*

If any key of the piano is struck and the tone prolonged by holding the key down— that is, by keeping the damper raised from the single string—as the tone dies away it loses not only in force but also in quality. But if the same key is struck while all the dampers are raised by the pedal, as the tone dies away it becomes richer and fuller, gathering into itself the sympathetic vibrations of all the strings to which it is related through its harmonic chord. Chopin's recognition of the effects to be obtained from this use of the pedal enabled him to add the charm of increased tonal beauty to his seductive melodies and fascinating harmonies; and these effects have

---
* See Introduction.

become the common property of all later composers for the piano-forte.

Chopin's playing was characterized by a novel freedom of rhythm, which he often indicated by the direction 'tempo rubato'—in consequence of which he has suffered so much at the hands of sentimental amateurs. Of this, his own peculiarly characteristic manner of performance, it has been said that "the measure wavered, rose and fell like a flame touched with the living breath." Liszt compares it to tree-tops stirred by the breeze while their trunks are still immovably rooted in the ground. Rubato playing is one of those artistic inexactitudes which in all departments distinguish the superstructure of art from its foundation of mathematics—too slight to impair the accuracy of the outline, yet imparting life and warmth to the cold calculation of the design.

To Franz Liszt is due the present amazing development of piano-forte virtuosity. The stories of his performances and of the charm by which he held his hearers spellbound read almost like the ancient myths that tell of the miraculous power of tone. The immense development which the art of piano-forte playing received at his hands brought about a complete revolution in technique, in the literature, and in the construction of the instrument itself; his enormous muscular force, which would have annihilated the instruments of an earlier day, necessitating an increased power of resistance in all parts of the mechanism. Liszt's compositions are full of technical and tonal effects which, though familiar to the present generation, were in his day entirely novel. In fingering he scarcely recognizes any difference between the black and white keys, using the thumb and little finger as freely upon one as upon the other. For trills in double thirds or sixths or octaves he often uses both hands. His transcriptions of violin passages exhibit technical figures never before applied to the piano, and in his arrangements of orchestral works he expands the chords to such impossible dimensions as to compel the passing of one hand over the other for the extreme tones—making their successful performance possible only by a skilful use of the pedal. The majority of Liszt's special effects depend upon the co-operation of the pedal, and through his utilization of what was long considered an almost useless part of the instrument, he opened many new possibilities to composers. What an important factor the pedal is in modern piano-forte playing we all know, but possibly we do not realize how it has revolutionized the style of composing for that instrument. Its use as illustrated in Liszt's transcriptions and arrangements so multiplies, as it were, the fingers of the player that every note of a whole orchestral score may be represented on the key-board; and all later composers of piano-forte music have profited by Liszt's revelation of the possibilities of the damper pedal.

It is difficult to imagine a development of piano-forte technique beyond that represented by Liszt's performance and demanded by his compositions. In a letter written at the height of his fame he says: "It remains my firm resolution to renounce the piano-forte only when I shall have accomplished on it all that is possible for me to accomplish in my day." Could it be that when Liszt closed his career as a virtuoso he felt that he had indeed developed to the utmost the resources of the piano-forte and accomplished upon it all that was possible even to his genius? None of the disciples he trained in the school at Weimar have reached the height upon which the master stood; the greatest players known to the present generation have gone no farther, and it seems indeed impossible that piano-forte virtuosity—save by the aid of improved mechanical appliances, such as new key-boards which remove or lessen physical impediments—should ever be developed beyond the point at which Liszt left it.

XI

The Orchestra

THE highest and most perfect exponent of absolute music—that is, music not associated with words—is the orchestra. In the ancient Greek theatre the orchestra was the semicircular space between the stage and the seats of the spectators, in which space dances and various evolutions were performed by the chorus to the accompaniment of musical instruments; and the corresponding space in a modern theatre is still called the orchestra. But in modern usage the word orchestra is chiefly applied to a body of performers upon instruments among which those of the violin family predominate;* and, collectively, to the instruments upon which they play.

---

* A body of performers using principally wind instruments is generally called a band.

The Orchestra

The instruments of the orchestra are usually disposed according to the following plan:

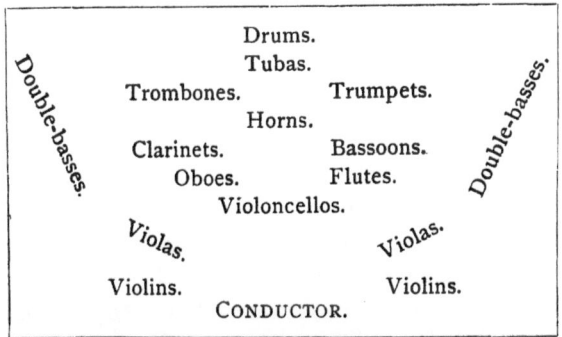

Though the arrangement is arbitrary and varies somewhat under different conductors, yet the same general plan is always followed: the stringed instruments in front and on the sides, the reeds, or wood-wind, instruments in the centre, and the brass and drums at the back. The orchestra, aside from the instruments of percussion, naturally divides itself into three distinct groups—strings, woodwinds and brass-winds. In each of these groups the tone quality appears, as it were, in different shades of the same tint, and each group is complete in itself and capable of expressing perfect and independent harmony.

The strings—that is, the instruments of the violin family in their four sizes, violins, violas, violoncellos and double or contra-basses—are the most important of these groups. All these instruments are constructed upon the same principle and played in the same manner; the strings are set in vibration by means of a bow held in the right hand, while the pitch of the tone is fixed by stopping, or shortening the vibrating length of the string, with the fingers of the left. In all stringed instruments the open tone of the lowest string —that is, the tone obtained from the whole length of the string, without stopping—is, of course, the lowest tone of the instrument;  the highest tone depends very much upon the skill of the player. The range of the strings in an orchestra is from EE, the lowest tone of the double-bass, to about $\bar{\bar{g}}$ of the violin, though the violin can produce tones beyond this which are not unfrequently required for the performance of orchestral compositions. In a string quartet the four parts or voices—soprano, alto, tenor and bass—are represented by the first and second violins, viola and violoncello, and in orchestral music the double-bass often merely plays the 'cello part an octave lower.

The quartet of wood-winds consists of flute, oboe, clarinet and bassoon. The flute, in its form of small octave flute, or piccolo, provides the highest tones of the orchestra—reaching to A in altissimo.

The music for the piccolo is usually, for convenience, written an octave lower than it is intended to sound; the instrument transposing it to the desired pitch.

The clarinet, oboe and bassoon are all reed instruments; that is, their tones are produced by the vibration of reeds—thin slips of cane —inserted in the mouth-piece and set in motion by the breath of the player. The somewhat nasal quality of their tones is frequently characterized as reedy. The clarinet and oboe are much alike in shape and size, but the tone of the former is produced by a single vibrating reed, while the oboe is played with a double reed—that is, two thin slips of cane bound together and attached to a short projecting tube of metal.

The clarinet, which produces some of the most beautiful tones of the orchestra, is one of the most difficult instruments to play. It is very susceptible to atmospheric variations, easily put out of tune and difficult to change

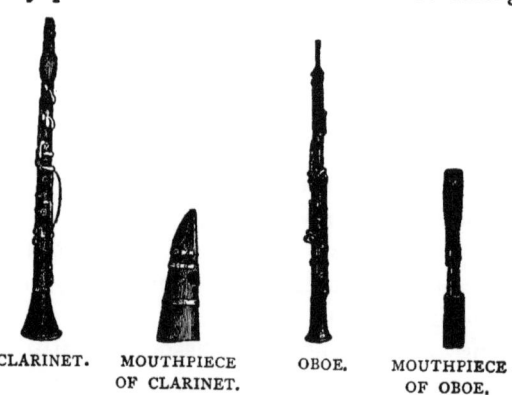

CLARINET.   MOUTHPIECE   OBOE.   MOUTHPIECE
            OF CLARINET.   OF OBOE.

in respect to pitch. Because of the difficulty of producing the semitones, different clarinets are used for different keys. Three are commonly used in the orchestra: one in C, for the natural key; one in B flat, for flat keys; and one in A, for sharp keys. Since the scale of the B flat clarinet provides for two flats, in the scale of E flat, for example, only one would need to be artificially produced, instead of three, as would be the case if the clarinet in C—the natural scale—were used; and, in like manner, the clarinet in A provides for three sharps, lessening by so many the number of those to be artificially produced in scales requiring a greater number. The mechanism is the same in all, but the pitch, or range of sounds, is different. The note C will on the C clarinet sound as written, but on the B flat clarinet C will sound B flat, and on the A clarinet C will sound A. Therefore, the part for the B flat clarinet is written a tone higher than it is intended to sound; that for the A clarinet a tone and a half (a minor third) higher; and the clarinet to be used is indicated by the composer—the instrument transposing the tones to the required pitch. So that a melody in E flat played by the B flat clarinet would be written in the key of F. It is just as if the piano should be tuned a whole tone too low; then an accompaniment to a song in the key of C would have to be written and played in the key of D, according to the key-board; or, if it were tuned a tone and a half (a minor third) too low—corresponding to the clarinet in A—an accompaniment to a song in the key of C would have to be written and played in E flat.

The corno di bassetto, or basset horn, is a clarinet of lower range and fuller tone, which sounds every note a fifth lower than it is written; its part, therefore, is always written a fifth higher than it is intended to be heard. The cor anglais, or English horn, stands in the same relation to the ordinary oboe, and is written for accordingly.

The bassoon, which is a double-reed instrument, is the natural bass of the wood-wind quartet. The double or contra-bassoon bears the same relation to it that the double-bass does to the violoncello, ranging an octave lower.

The brass instruments commonly used in the orchestra are horns, trumpets, trombones and tubas. The tones which these instruments naturally produce are the harmonics of the lowest or fundamental tone,* and these, which are called the open tones of the instrument, are obtained by simply blowing with greater or less force into the mouthpiece. For the other tones of the scale it is necessary to partially close the aperture of the bell—as in the horn—or to modify the length of the tube;

---
* See Introduction.

either by piercing the side with holes which are provided with keys—as in the flute and clarinet; or by sliding one portion of the tube into the other—as in the trombone; or by pistons—which are sections of tubes moved up and down by keys. In addition, the tube itself can be more or less lengthened by means of movable pieces called crooks, and so the instrument tuned to any desired pitch.

The French horn is perhaps the most characteristic of this group of instruments. It was originally a hunting horn, and when first introduced into the orchestra was condemned as coarse and vulgar. To soften the tone a pad or damper was inserted in the bell of the instrument, when it was discovered that partially closing the aperture raised the pitch. From this originated the method of playing with the hand in the bell, and by stopping with the fingers obtaining the intermediate tones of the harmonic scale. The tube of the horn is sixteen feet in length; its natural key is C, and its part is always written in

C. It can be made to play in other keys, however, by the addition of crooks, which by changing the length of the tube change its pitch; and the composer indicates what crook is to be used—that is, in what key the horns are to play.

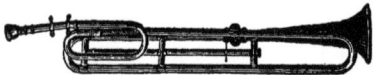

The trumpet, like the horn, produces naturally only the tones of the harmonic series; but by means of modern contrivances—valves, etc.—the intermediate tones may be obtained, and the pitch may be changed by the addition of crooks.

The tones of the trombone, which has slides

shortening or lengthening its tube, are not fixed, but, as with stringed instruments, depend upon the player, who, guided by his ear, can produce upon it any interval within its compass. Therefore it is not usually played from transposed parts, like the horn, clarinet and other instruments, but the real notes are written.

Tubas are the bass instruments of the sax-horn family — so called from a celebrated manufacturer and inventor of musical instruments named Sax. They are the largest of the brass, and are all furnished with valves and made in many keys. Indeed, every brass instrument now used in the orchestra is provided with some contrivance which enables it to produce all the 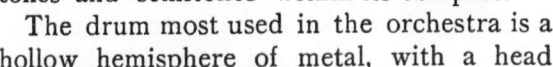tones and semitones within its compass.

The drum most used in the orchestra is a hollow hemisphere of metal, with a head of vellum fitted over a ring having screws which serve to tighten or slacken the head, and so raise or lower the pitch.

There are usually two kettle-drums in an orchestra, tuned to tonic and dominant of the key; generally the dominant a fourth below the tonic, but sometimes that a fifth above, and occasionally the drums are tuned to the tonic and its octave. Sometimes more kettledrums, or drums tuned at other intervals, are used in order to avoid changing the key—an operation which requires considerable time, as all the screws have to be turned in succession,* and also a very nice perception of pitch on the part of the drummer; since the drum must often be tuned to one key while the rest of the instruments are still playing in another.

We do not sufficiently appreciate those humbler members of the orchestra whose conscientious co-operation enables us to enjoy the great works of the great composers. When we have listened with delight to a symphony of Beethoven or Schumann, or to a music drama of Wagner, do we ever think of the long hours of monotonous practice necessary to evoke the deep, full tones of the bassoon—of the swollen and blistered lips which are the first reward of the horn player. —of the care and skill necessary to produce correctly the single tones of those instru-

---

* Owing to the uneven texture of the vellum mechanical devices for turning the screws simultaneously have not proved very successful.

SEVENTH SYMPHONY.

Dem Reichsgrafen Moritz von Fries gewidmet.

CONDUCTOR'S ORCHESTRAL SCORE.

ments which have no independent part to play, but merely enhance the effect and beauty of the whole? It would seem at first thought as if nothing could be simpler than to tap the drum at the first beat of the measure—but just think a moment! When the bâton of the conductor is raised to give the signal for beginning, every bow is ready on the string, the mouth-piece of every wind instrument at the lips of the player; but the drummer has his stick poised in the air, so far away from the head of the drum that if it were to begin to descend at the moment the conductor's signal is given, the sound would be heard *after* the other instruments and throw the whole orchestra into confusion; so that the drummer really has to learn to play out of time—to anticipate, as it were, the beat of the conductor. While we revere the genius of the composer and admire the power of the leader let us also appreciate the skill and devotion of the obscure performers whose patient practice upon difficult and thankless instruments alone makes it possible for the one to translate for us into audible language the thoughts of the other.

From very early times instruments have

been used not only singly but also in combination. Egyptian mural paintings show bands of instrumental performers under leaders, and in ancient literature are frequent allusions to instruments of different kinds which seem to indicate that they were used together. But from what we know of ancient music it is almost certain that these instruments all played the same melody in unison—or perhaps an octave apart, according to their range—and that real concerted music was unknown.

For about a thousand years of its European development also music was strictly unisonal; but after the invention of counterpoint vocal compositions gradually became more and more elaborate and intricate, until finally, in the sixteenth century, stringed instruments came to be used in secular compositions as an aid to the voices. These instruments, viols of different sizes, simply played each in unison with the corresponding voice. When a voice was lacking the part was represented by the instrument alone, or, sometimes, only one part was sung while all the others were played; and the performance of such compositions entirely by instruments, without voices, was really the beginning of modern concerted music and the germ from which the orchestra has been developed. Even, however, after instrumental music was recognized as a separate branch of art, the manner of writing for instruments was exactly the same as for unaccompanied voices; and to the end of the sixteenth century the instruments by which the parts were to be played were not specified by the composer. The director simply distributed the parts according to the compass of the instruments at his disposition, without any regard to the quality of their tones. For a long while, also, the different classes of instruments were kept separate, being used in alternation instead of in combination; so that even a great array of instruments could scarcely be termed an orchestra.

The history of orchestration really begins with the seventeenth century. Orchestration, instrumentation, scoring—terms which are virtually synonymous—mean the manner in which the various instruments of the orchestra are employed by the composer, as indicated in his written score, to produce the tonal effects desired. Different styles of orchestration may mean either a different selection of instruments, or a different mode of treating the same selection of instruments, or both; and the present aim is briefly to trace the gradual progress of this branch of musical art from its first crude beginnings to its present splendid development, as illustrated in the works of Wagner and Tschaikowsky.

The first oratorio, 'L'Anima e Corpo,' by Emilio del Cavaliere, which was performed at Rome in the year 1600, was accompanied by a viol di gamba, a harpsichord, a double guitar and two flutes. This little band was kept entirely out of sight, like Wagner's orchestra at Bayreuth. At Florence, in the same year, the first opera, 'Euridice,' by Jacopo Peri, was accompanied by a harpsichord, a viol di gamba, a large guitar and a large lute; these instruments also were hidden from the view of the audience. But less than ten years later Monteverde employed for the accompaniment of 'Orfeo' no less than thirty-five instruments; a heterogeneous array, which, however, he used with considerable skill. Monteverde (1566–1650) may really be regarded as the father of the modern art of orchestration. He was the first to perceive that the tone-quality of the different instruments may be used as a means of expression; and the varying combinations of instruments with the changes in the dramatic situation in 'Orfeo' are, Ambros says, the first attempts at instrumentation.

In the seventeenth century dramatic music made rapid progress, and the composition of the orchestra gradually became settled and more orderly. The principal instruments were viols of various kinds; the thoroughbass being played by the largest and the chords filled out on the harpsichord, which was always the centre of the early orchestra. Until the custom of beating time with a bâton was established—that is, until the present century—the conductor always presided at the harpsichord; not unfrequently—in deference to distinguished listeners in the audience—with his back to the musicians. The modern conductor plays upon his orchestra as a virtuoso does upon his instrument. He endeavors to grasp the inner meaning of the composer, and so to control the hundred instruments at his command as perfectly to interpret to the audience his individual conception of the composition. But before Beethoven's day conducting was merely timekeeping; which, indeed, was all that was necessary for the music to be rendered.

Before the close of the century the violin had become the leading instrument, and composers had learned to use the string quartet, the foundation of the orchestra, almost exactly as it is used to-day. The first wind instruments added to the strings seem to have been oboes and bassoons—both of which the older composers used in far greater numbers than we ever hear at the present time—but horns, trumpets and flutes soon followed. The wind instruments were at first used merely to give greater fulness of tone by playing in unison with the strings, but in the scores of Bach (1685–1750) and Händel (1685–1759) they begin to have real parts and often long, independent solo passages.

At first the orchestral overture or symphony was known only in connection with the drama. The word symphony had no definite signification in regard to form, but was applied to any purely instrumental portions of a vocal work. Introductions, interludes and dances were alike termed symphonies; the overture being distinguished as the 'Sinfonia avanti l'Opera.' These instrumental passages were not considered very important, and composers had small encouragement to bestow much labor or pains upon this portion of their work. Dr. Burney tells how little attention the 'people of quality' gave to the music of an opera, aside from some favorite air or the performance of a celebrated singer. He says : " The music at the theatres in Italy seems but an excuse for people to assemble together, their attention being chiefly placed on play and conversation even during the performance of a serious opera ;"—for the gaming-tables were an inseparable adjunct of the opera-house, and the impressario of the latter was often also the lessee of the former. Naturally, therefore, composers did not expend much labor upon the instrumental portions of their works, and it was not until the so-called symphonies began to be played as separate pieces in concerts that we find any real development of the art of orchestration.

These 'independent symphonies' became extremely popular, and great numbers of them were composed in the first half of the eighteenth century. They are generally scored for two violins, viola and violoncello, a pair of oboes, or flutes, and two horns. These early symphonies, which were almost as frequently styled overtures, were in one movement only—or, rather, in three connected movements. It was Haydn (1732-1809) who separated the three movements and interpolated a fourth—the minuet.

Haydn's first symphonies were written for the earlier little group of instruments—the four strings, two oboes and two horns—but as new instruments were invented or old ones improved he gradually added others and began experiments in grouping them to produce new effects. Haydn's great influence upon the development of orchestration was largely due to the opportunities afforded by his long connection with the extensive musical establishment maintained by Prince Esterhazy. He is somewhere described as making experiments in instrumentation and ringing the bell for the band to come and try them, and though this is doubtless an exaggeration, he certainly enjoyed unusual facilities for testing his works.

But Haydn probably would not have reached his highest development without the influence of Mozart (1756–91), his brilliant contemporary. Mozart, who was but three years old when Haydn wrote his first symphony, was, very naturally, at first much under his influence. "It was from Haydn," said he, "that I learned the true way to compose quartets." But Mozart's precocious genius rapidly outran the older composer, and Haydn's best symphonies, the works of his old age, show plainly the influence of Mozart. Haydn and Mozart, who together fixed the form of the symphony, did much also for the development of orchestration. In their compositions the wind instruments, instead of being entirely subordinated to the strings, excepting in distinctly solo passages, become more independent, are treated more characteristically, and used to provide effects of contrast rather than merely increased strength of tone. In the works of Haydn and Mozart the balance between wind and strings is first definitely established.*

In the eighteenth century a symphony was a very slight work—composers wrote them by the dozen. The standard of performance was extremely rough and audiences not critical, and it was not thought either unjust to the work or disrespectful to the composer to divide a symphony, playing one-half at the beginning of a concert and the other half at the close. The length, as well as the composition of the programmes, excites our wonder. Three symphonies, a couple of overtures, a concerto and half a dozen smaller

---

* It was Mozart who introduced the clarinet into the orchestra. In one of his letters he says: "You cannot imagine the splendid effect of a symphony with flutes, oboes and clarinets."

pieces were not unusual, and concerts sometimes lasted four or five hours. When Beethoven's fourth symphony was first produced it was preceded by all the other three; and even such great works as these were often given in public with very insufficient preparation. Orchestral music has never been so well performed as it is to-day.

Haydn, who wrote his first symphony when such a composition was of little more importance than a string quartet, lived to hear Beethoven's 'Eroica'—an immense development to be spanned by one lifetime. Beethoven (1770–1827) greatly expanded the form of the symphony, and developed the art of orchestration with indefatigable effort. Such a worker as Beethoven the world has rarely seen. His sketch-books bear record to the devotion with which he labored at his compositions; some portions of his works being rewritten from a dozen to twenty times. From the first he used clarinets; he introduced the trombone into the symphonic orchestra and increased the number of the horns to four. He was the first to use the drum as an independent instrument, instead of merely to mark the rhythm, and another innovation was his use of both drums together in chords. He also subdivided the strings, which before his day had seldom been used in any other than regular four-part harmony. Beethoven acquired a wonderful command of the orchestra, and his compositions abound in new combinations and tonal effects as novel as beautiful.

Weber (1786–1826), who used the orchestra most successfully in connection with the drama, was an instrumentalist of the first rank. He gave an increased independence to the wood-wind choir, to which are largely due the marvellous effects, now weird and mysterious, now exquisitely fairylike, of his lovely overtures. Schubert (1797–1828) and Mendelssohn (1809–47) also produced novel and delightful effects with the wind instruments. Berlioz (1803–69), who wrote a treatise on instrumentation which no composer neglects to study, acquired such a command of the orchestra that, as one writer has said, he played upon it as Paganini on the violin or Liszt on the piano-forte.

It was Richard Wagner's intimate acquaintance with all the resources of the orchestra which, guided by his instinct for dramatic effect, enabled him to use it with such unprecedented success for the expression of the most subtle fancies and daring flights of his genius. He largely increased the number of instruments, especially of wind instruments, and to him is chiefly due the introduction of the deepest toned of the group of brass; but the exceptional array of instruments in his scores is not merely for increased tonal power, but far more for the production of special effects. He completes each group of wind instruments by the addition of others of lower range, so as to get full chords from each group without mixture of timbre; and he often uses his most imposing array of brass for the production of piano and pianissimo effects.

Since the time of Haydn and Mozart the general principles upon which the standard orchestra is composed have been definitely established. Now, as then, the orchestral forces consist of strings, wood-winds, brass-winds and instruments of percussion; and of these the stringed band forms the foundation, while the others are used both in combination and in contrast. But the art of orchestration has undergone countless modifications. Every new instrument introduced into the orchestra and every improvement either in compass, quality of tone, or executive powers of the instruments already in use, make possible and result in an endless variety of new combinations.

During the past two centuries stringed instruments have suffered little change, but, with the exception of the trombone and bassoon, every wind instrument has been completely metamorphosed. The wood-winds have become more powerful in tone and more true in pitch, and the scale of the brass-winds has been completed by the introduction of valves. The capacity of stringed instruments, also, has been greatly increased by the superior technique of modern orchestral players, who are to-day expected to execute what would have been considered bravura passages for solo players a hundred years ago.

But the manner of writing for instruments has changed far more than the instruments themselves. Instead of being used only in distinct groups, these are now combined and subdivided in almost every conceivable way. Prior to Beethoven the strings were used almost without exception only in four-part harmony—in 'Tristan and Isolde' Wagner divides the violins alone into sixteen separate groups. On the other hand, where the older composers would have dispersed the strings among three or four parts of the harmony Wagner often concentrates nearly all of them upon a single part; balancing in this way an increased number of wind instruments, the proportion of which in the modern orchestra is often nearly double what it was in Beethoven's day.

The greater power and brilliancy of the modern orchestra are not due solely to the employment of a greater number of instruments. They are in a much larger measure the result of an increased knowledge of the use of those instruments, and the opportunities which improvements in their mechanism afford the composer.

A distinguished man once refused to let his son study music upon the ground that it is an unintellectual pursuit. On the other hand, a well-known critic says that the score of one of Wagner's music-dramas seems to him the highest achievement of the human intellect. It certainly cannot be denied that music may be, indeed, often is, studied after an unintellectual fashion; but it is equally certain that no one can master even the mechanical details of orchestration—the qualities and capabilities of the different instruments, the methods of writing in the various clefs and the transpositions necessary for the wind instruments—without a very high degree of intellectual capacity, leaving entirely out of consideration the question of musical talent or genius. And when we remember that, having mastered all these mechanical details, the composer works, not like the painter or sculptor from carefully selected models, but absolutely originates his own ideas, evolves and develops them entirely from his own inner consciousness, it seems impossible to deny that the creation of a great orchestral work is an achievement of the highest intellect combined with the greatest genius.

For the privilege of reproducing the illustrations of rare old instruments in the collection of Mr. Morris Steinert, New Haven, Conn., the author is indebted to the courtesy of the owner.

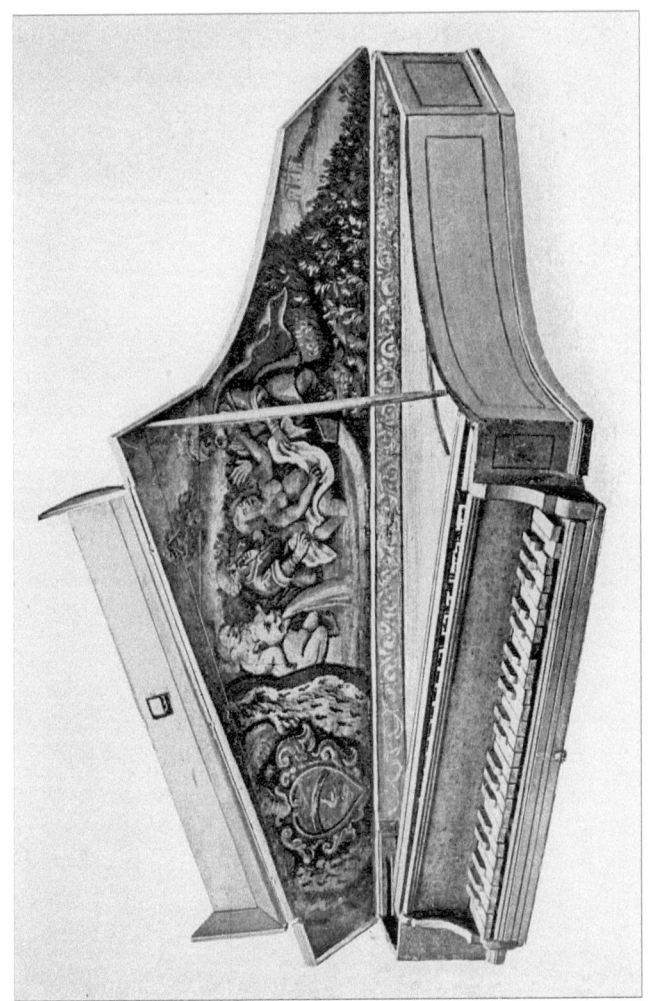

ITALIAN SPINET (FIFTEENTH CENTURY).
Steinert Collection.

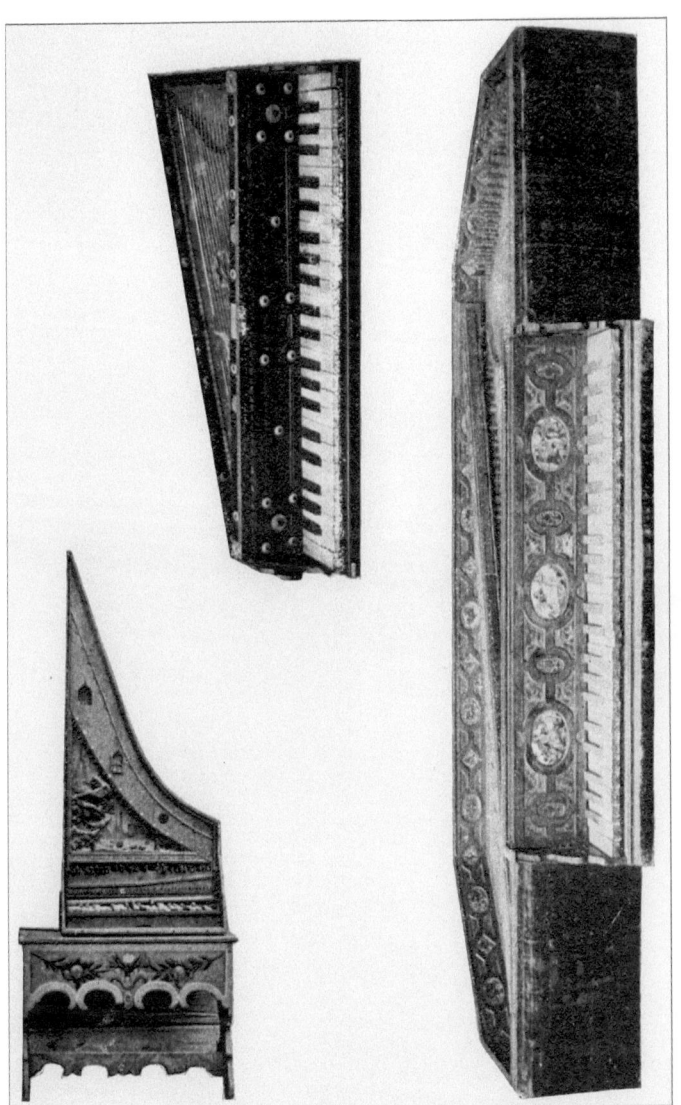

OLD ITALIAN INSTRUMENTS.

ITALIAN VIRGINAL (SIXTEENTH CENTURY).
South Kensington Museum.

ITALIAN SPINET (SIXTEENTH CENTURY).
South Kensington Museum.

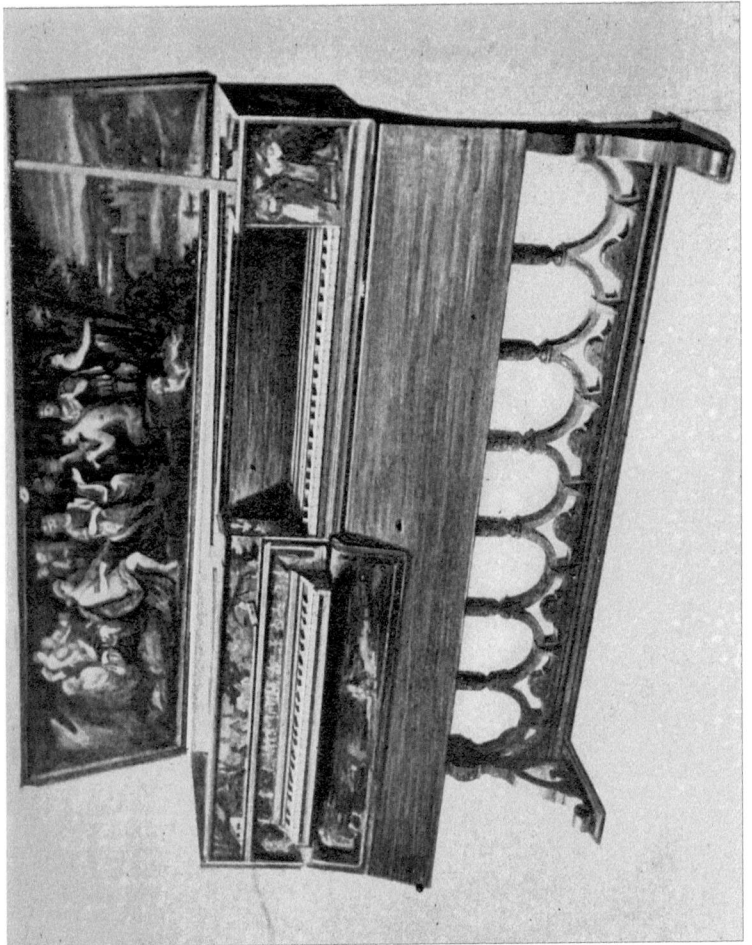

DOUBLE SPINET (END OF SIXTEENTH CENTURY).
Steinert Collection.

HARPSICHORD (END OF SIXTEENTH CENTURY).
Museum of the Paris Conservatory.

CLAVICHORD (SEVENTEENTH CENTURY).
Steinert Collection.

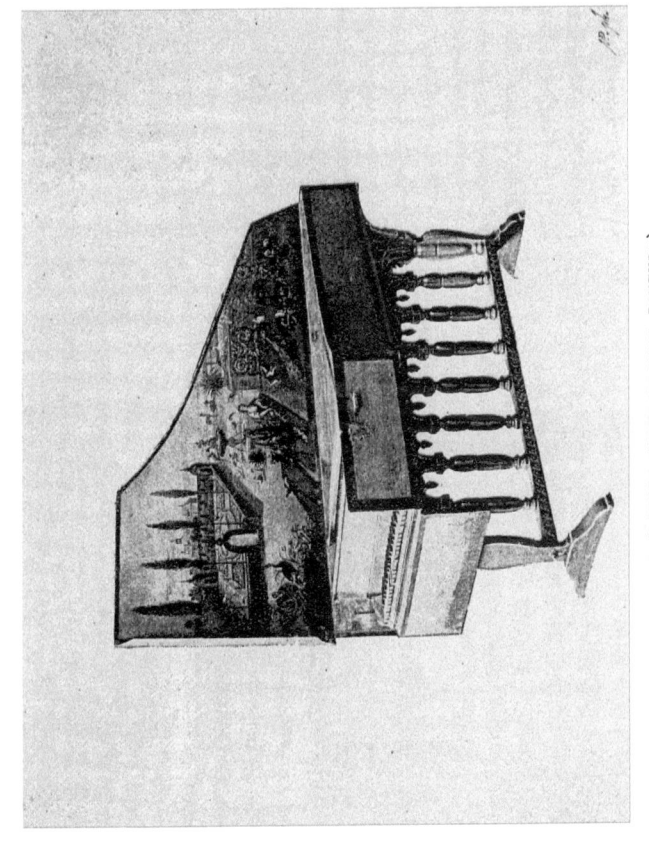

HARPSICHORD (SEVENTEENTH CENTURY).
Steinert Collection.

ENGLISH SPINET (ABOUT 1750).
Steinert Collection.

Index

INDEX

ÆOLIAN scale, 23
Allemande, 135
Alternativo, 136
Answer, of fugue, 132
Arabian scale, 75
Aria, 92, 97, 98
Artificial voices, 97
Authentic modes, 27 *et seq.*

BACH, C. P. E., 145, 168, 186
Bach, J. S., 62, 118, 119, 163, 183, 184, 218
Bar, 47 *et seq.*
Basso continuo, 179, 180
Bassoon, 206
Bebung, 168
Beethoven, 103, 120, 141, 146, 147, 190, 222, 223, 225
Berlioz, 223
Binary form, 141, 145
Bourree, 136

CANON, 62 *et seq.*; cancrizans, 64
Canto fermo, 57
Cavalieri, Emilio del, 114
Cavalli, 91
Chaconne, 137
Cherubini, 102
Chest of viols, 125

Chopin, 194 *et seq.*
Chorale, 117
Chords of the seventh and ninth, 89
Christofori, Bartolomei, 170
Clarinet, 203 *et seq.*, 221, 222
Classical music, 104; composers, 105
Claveçin, 165
Clavichord, 148 *et seq.*, 185; gebunden, 153; bundfrei, 153
Clavier, 123
Clefs, 35
Clementi, 189
Close and half-close, 129
Coda, 140
Conducting, 217
Contrapuntal music, 55 *et seq.*
Cor anglais, 206
Corno di bassetto, 205
Counterpoint, 55 *et seq.*
Couperin, 183, 184
Courante, 136

DISCANT, 56, 57
Dissonance, prepared, 90
Dorian scale, 22
Dot, 47, 48
Dufay, Guillaume, 62
Dulcimer, 170

Index

EAR, 11
Ecclesiastical scales, 28, 79 *et seq.*
Enharmonic, 24, 162
Episode, 133, 142
Exposition of fugue, 132; of sonata, 138

FANTASIA, or free part, 138, 139
Field, John, 192
Figured bass, 179, 180
Fingering, 180 *et seq.*, 184, 187, 194, 197
First movement form, 137; plan of, 138; in minor, 139; in early sonatas, 145
Flute, 203
Force of musical tone, 6
Form in music, 127 *et seq.*
Franco of Cologne, 45
Fugue, 131 *et seq.*; plan of, 134
Fundamental bass, 94, 95

GAVOTTE, 136
Gigue, 136
Gluck, 98 *et seq.*
Greek music, 20 *et seq.*; drama, 20, 83; scales, 21 *et seq.*; notation, 21, 33
Ground bass, 137
Guerre des Bouffons, 95, 96
Guido d' Arezzo, 37 *et seq.*, 151

HÄNDEL, 62, 118, 218
Harmonic chord, 7
Harmonics, 6 *et seq.*; influence upon tone, 9
Harpsichord, 148, 163 *et seq.*, 185, 217

Haydn, 119, 120, 141, 145, 188, 219 *et seq.*
Hearing, 11 *et seq.*
Hebrew music, 19
Hexachord, 40 *et seq.*
Homophonic music, 70, 84, 85
Horn, 207, 222
Hucbaldus, 36, 56
Hungarian scale, 77
Hymn, 116, 117

IMITATIONS, 132
Instruments, earliest, 18; of orchestra, 201
Intermezzo, 95
Ionian scale, 23
Italian opera, origin of, 84

JACK, 148, 163
Josquin des Prés, 65, 66

KEISER, 93
Kettledrum, 209, 222
Kuhnau, 144

LASSUS, 67
Leading motives, 109
Leading note, 80, 81
Liszt, 194, 196 *et seq.*
Locrian scale, 23
Lulli, 93, 94
Lute, 122, 123
Lydian scale, 23

MADRIGAL, 69, 70, 125
Measured chant, 45
Meistersinger, 52
Mendelssohn, 120, 194, 223
Merulo, Claudio, 176

Index 253

Meyerbeer, 102
Minnesinger, 52
Minstrels, 50
Minuet, 136, 141
Mixolydian scale, 23
Monochord, 149, 150, 152, 154
Monodic music, 70, 84, 85
Monteverde, 88 et seq., 216
Motive, 130
Mozart, 101, 102, 145, 188, 220, 221
Music, in nature, 15; printing, 66
Musical form, 127

NEUMÆ, 33
Notation, 32 et seq.
Notes, 45, 46

OBOE, 203
Orchestration, 215, 224 et seq.
Organ, 30 et seq.; point, 133
Organum, 56
Oriental music, 6 et seq.
Overture, 94

PALESTRINA, 70 et seq.
Partial tones, 6 et seq.
Partita, 135 et seq.
Passecaille, 137
Passion music, 118
Pedal, 169, 195, 197, 198; point, 133
Pentatonic scale, 76 et seq.
Peri, 88
Period, 128
Phrygian scale, 23
Piano-forte, 170 et seq.; 190
Piccolo, 203
Pitch of musical tone, 5

Plagal modes, 27 et seq.
Plain-chant, 47
Plain-song, 32
Polyphonic music, 70, 85, 131
Primary form, 141
Programmes, 221
Psaltery, 161, 163
Purcell, 93

QUALITY of musical tone, 6

RAMEAU, 94, 160
Romantic opera, 104; music, 104; composers, 105
Rondo, 142
Rossini, 103
Rubato playing, 196

SARABANDE, 136
Scarlatti, Alessandro, 92
Scarlatti, Domenico, 183
Scherzo, 141
Schubert, 223
Schumann, 194
Schütz, 93
Score, 48; orchestral, 211
Section, 129
Sequence, 130
Silbermann, 171, 172
Slow movement, 141
Solmization, 13
Sonata, 137 et seq.; da chiesa, 143; da camera, 143
Sonatina, 139
Song-form, 141
Sound waves, 3, 4
Spinet, 148, 164
Spontini, 102
Stretto, 133

Strings, 202, 223, 225
Subject, 128; of fugue, 131
Suite, 135 *et seq.*
Symphony, 137, 218
Syren, 5

TABLATURE, 48, 49
Tangent, 149, 164
Temperament, 156 *et seq.*
Tetrachord, 21
Thalberg, 193
Thoroughbass, 179, 180
Time signatures, 46, 47
Triads, 89
Trio, 136
Trombone, 208, 221

Troubadours, 50 *et seq.*
Trumpet, 208
Tuba, 209

VECCHI, Orazio, 86
Verdi, 103
Viol, 123 *et seq.*, 214
Virginal, 164
Volkslied, 105, 106, 117

WAGNER, 106 *et seq.*, 223, 224, 225
Weber, 104 *et seq.*, 223
Willaert, 69
Working out, 138

ZARLINO, 81, 158

For EU product safety concerns, contact us at Calle de José Abascal, 56–1°,
28003 Madrid, Spain or eugpsr@cambridge.org.

www.ingramcontent.com/pod-product-compliance
Ingram Content Group UK Ltd.
Pitfield, Milton Keynes, MK11 3LW, UK
UKHW041951230426
12048UKWH00008B/269